ARABS

ALL YOU NEED TO KNOW

Michel Sedaghat

To Alexander, Xavier and Jean Pierre

ISBN 978-1-4457-6512-9

2

Preface

"Arabs, All you need to know" is a cross cultural handbook intended to be read, effortlessly and quickly, by people who are not specialists of Arab cultural and historical studies. The purpose of this book is to assist you to understand the complexity, beauty and diversity of the Arab way of life. This includes socio-cultural, religious, and political interactions that have created the basis of the word Arab.

In modern society, the term Arab is so broadly used that many people around the world assume that they are all the same people. Typically, Arabs are stereotyped because of their similar religious beliefs, characteristics and languages. However, Arab is a very general term, similar to the word European. The term Arab refers to an ethnicity, but not all Arabic speaking people.

I've decided to write this handbook about Arabs and the powerful personality of Arabia to create a bridge between the Arab community and the rest of the world. It is a reconnaissance of the Arabic traditions, history and essence of Arabian life. Over the last 7 years I have lived among the Arabic customs, and have become overwhelmed with unanswered questions. Those questions needed to be answered, and with the concept that others might need the same information, I chose to write my findings in this book.

Before we continue, I urge you to put your preconceived notions aside. Regardless of your origins or cultural belongings, the focus here is to learn more about the Arabs and Arabia. This book is designed to expand your knowledge with what I have learned. Granted, my views may be incorporated in portions of this handbook, but they will be shared through various questions and answers. Some that will certainly provoke questions of your own.

What you will notice is that with this handbook contains many of the basic five questions types. They are Who, What, Where, When, Why and the non-traditional How. All my questions have been chosen carefully as they represent truly the Arab way of life and wonderful individuality of Arabia. These answers will enable you to share the knowledge in a simple and easily understood manner with your friends and families.

While I could focus on technical details and complex historical information, I chose to skip that and focus my information more on the interesting aspects of culture and lifestyles. It is my intention to explore areas that may help you understand this culture as a whole rather than being a history lesson.

It should also be mentioned that I do touch on Islamic beliefs in this handbook as well. With this information, I hope you find it has been handled with respect and esteem which is vital in the understanding of the Arabic daily life. Also included is information on the Arabic language and Arabs combined with Islam, as this is key in understanding the Arabian Peninsula's history and traditions.

No information provided is intended to be presented in a malicious intent to the reader. It is being written with respect for the culture as a whole. Any mistakes in this written are purely coincidental and not intended. My interpretations of history and culture are meant only to educate others about this amazing and diverse people.

In closing this section, I would like to provide you with some interesting facts:

- In the modern world, there are 17 Arabs countries, while 22 countries are members of the Arab League.
- Muslims are a religious majority in 55 countries around the world.
- In the present time there are more than 323 million Arabs, 5 percent of which are Christians or other religions.
- There are 1.5 billion Muslims in the world and without a doubt; Islam is the fastest growing religion. Islam is the second largest faith in both the United States and Europe.

Dates and Historical Facts

I think I should mention here that many books will refer to historical facts based on the Christian Calendar. This calendar uses the year Christ was born as the dividing year. In modern society this is typically the most recognized and acknowledged reference for modern events. Understandably, people all over the world no matter their religious beliefs, ethnicity or language understand the Christian calendar.

I am sure you have seen acronyms such as AD and BC in many books or articles. AD refers to Anno Domini, from the Latin language which stands for "The Year of the Lord". The lord in this case is Jesus Christ and is considered by the Christian calendar as the beginning of their Era. BC refers to "Before Christ" and covers all historical events prior to the Christian era.

This book is about Arabs, Islam and the Arabian Era. Unable to use the Hijri calendar, I decided to use the internationally recognized dating system which has no religious association.

Technically, I should be using the annotation A.H, from Latin word Anno Hegirae, the calendar designation for the Muslims and Islamic civilization.

1 A.H is equivalent to 622 CE (Or 622 AD) and represents the year that the Islamic Prophet Mohammad left his birthplace of Mecca to go to the city of Yathrib, today's Madinah in Saudi Arabia, where he established the first capital of the new Islamic religion.

I used the acronyms CE and BCE standing for, in order, "Common Era" and "Before Common Era". This internationally recognized dating methodology refers to the year Zero of the Christian calendar but does not mention Jesus Christ as a birth reference. The Common Era concept is currently used by many historians in order to disassociate religious and historical facts.

I hope the date references used in this book will allow you to understand and remember the interesting historical facts of the Arabian Era.

Quote:

"Whoever has no past, has neither present nor future"

H.H Shiekh Zayed Bin Sultan Al Nahyan

President, UAE (1971-2004)

9

Arabs, All you need to know.

CONTENT:

1. What is the meaning of "Arab"?
2. What are the origins of the Arabic Alphabet?
3. How many Arabic dialects do Arabs speak?
4. Why most pan-Arab flags have the same colours?
5. Why do Arabs greet with "Salam Aleikum"?
6. Why do Egyptians speak Arabic and not Egyptian?
7. Where did the name Egypt come from?
8. Are all Arabs Muslims?
9. Why do Arabs and Jews distrust each other?
10. Why does Al-Cohol sounds like it is from Arabic origin?
11. Why is alcohol forbidden in Islam?
12. What is the Arak?
13. What is a halal meal?
14. Where does Kebab come from?
15. Why do Arabs offer coffee instead of tea?
16. Why the Oryx is the sign of many Arabic Countries?
17. Why do Arabs hunt with Falcons?
18. Why are Arabian horses considered the best?
19. Why is the Qur'an is considered a mathematical wonder?
20. Why Arabic names are mostly without surname?
21. Why Muslim men can marry more than once?
22. Why do Arab women use henna on their body?
23. Why Muslim women are covered with a hijab?

24. Why Arab men cover their heads with a Khaffiyeh?
25. What is the difference between a Sheikh, Emir and Sultan?
26. Why do we weigh precious stones in the Carat?
27. Why Palm trees are important in the Arabian lifestyle?
28. What is the origin of Shisha?
29. Who is the Prophet Mohammad?
30. What is the difference between a Shia and Sunni Muslim?
31. Where does the name Dubai comes from?
32. Why is the Islamic Calendar different than the Christian Calendar?
33. Do Muslims believe in Angels?
34. Why do Muslims pray so much?
35. What is Ramadan?
36. Where is Mecca and why is it the symbol of Islam?
37. Who created Saudi Arabia?
38. What is a Masjid?
39. Where is Al Madinah?
40. Where is the smallest mainland of Arabic Country?
41. Where is the Oldest Arabian City?
42. Where is the Sahara?
43. What is Sahara History?

1. ■ What is the meaning of "Arab"?

The word *Arab* has an uncertain meaning. It is relatively unclear when the term first came into existence, and who began to call the Arabs by this term. However, everyone agrees that the word "Arab" pre-dates Islam.

During my research, I found the word *Arab* in various scripts that appeared in various time periods of history. From the information that was available to me, the earliest sources where the term *Arab* appeared was in various Persian ancient scripts under the Persian Empire King Nehemyah during the 5th century BCE. The word Arab is used in reference to some Nabataean tribes located in modern day Jordan.

It was during this same period, the Greek historian Herodotus (484-425 BCE) mentions the Arabs, apparently in reference to the Yemenite tribes. "*They revolt against every power,*" he says, "*which seeks to control their freedom or demean them*". For years, the personal freedom of the Arabs has inspired the great Greek and Latin writers.

The above two references use the word *Arab* as we know today. With this information increasing my interest, I decided to dig a little further. I found that there are some earlier Assyrian records, located in today's Iraq that mention the word *"Arabi"*, a tribe of the desert that may be connected with the Ishmaelites. However, there is no concrete proof that such a term has even any relationship with the word Arab.

In fact, according to Bible and Qur'an, Prophet Abraham had two wives: Sarah and Hagar. Each of these women provided him with a son. Ishmael from Hagar and Isaac from Sarah. Very often, the Ishmaelites are identified as Arab people although this is an over-simplification.

When you research the roots of the word you will find the following translation not only informational, but interesting:

1) ereb = mixture of peoples.
2) arabah = prairie, land or wilderness.

Both of these terms are appropriate to describe the Arabs. The name "Arabia" was given to the whole peninsula only around the first century BCE., as defined by the well known Diodorus of Sicily in his *Bibliotheca Historica* and by Strabo in his book called *"Geography"*. Many major geographical definitions as we know today from these two master books.

Arabia is a geographic definition of the Arab world and it is not directly related to the actual ethnicity of the people. Many of them declare to be of several kinds and refer themselves by their own tribal names.

Today, the Arabian Peninsula is the Arabs' homeland and the people that lived in this location in ancient times are the ancestors of the modern Arabs. In the Western world, Arabs are referred to as "the Muslims" regardless of their geographical location, ethnic origin or current nationality.

Additionally, as soon as a person speaks the Arabic language, they are immediately considered to be "Arab". This narrow western view of the Arabs is very common and mixes all kind of Arabs from Morocco to Oman.

In context, let's explore this concept. What if we were to say that everyone no matter if they are English, French, or German nationals are all the same as they are all Europeans. This would be a misconception of course, but branding everyone based on one similarity is what happens with Arabs.

The original idea of this book is to fight such statements and provide a comprehensive view of the Arab population, culture and traditions.

2 ■ Where are the origins of the Arabic Alphabet?

Due to the influence of Islam, the Arabic alphabet is one of the most widespread writing systems in the world. Arabic is found in large parts of Africa and Western and Central Asia, as well as in ethnic communities in East Asia and Europe. Today, the Arabic alphabet is also used by other civilizations to write their own languages, such as Persian, Pashto, Urdu and more.

Arabic inscriptions are most common after the birth of Islam, around 7th century CE, but the origin of the Arabic alphabet lies deeper in time. The earliest pre-Arabic texts are the "Hasaean inscriptions" of eastern Saudi Arabia, from the 8th century BCE. This would mean that origin of the Arabic language was 1000 years before the birth of Islam. Obviously, these scripts are not written in the classical Arabic but in a very similar Alphabet called Musnad. We can consider Musnad, which is written right to left, as the grandfather of Qur'anic Arabic alphabet.

The Arabic alphabet evolved from the Nabataean Aramaic script during the 1st century CE. The Nabataeans established a kingdom in what is modern-day Jordan from the 2nd century BCE. Nabataeans were truly Arabs! Many Stone inscriptions can be seen in Petra, the capital of the Nabataean kingdom (150 BCE to 100 CE) and in Damascus and Madinah, written by Bedouin and nomadic tribes of the Arabian desert.

With time, Nabataeans wrote their texts and scripts with what we can consider as Pre-Qur'anic Arabic. The Nabataeans, or the Kingdom of Petra, lasted until the year 106 CE, when they were conquered by the Romans. Nabataean inscriptions continued to be written until the 4th century CE. The Nabataean alphabet had 28 letters and was written from right to left similar to the Qur'anic Arabic.

During the 7th century the Arabic alphabet was revised in order to remove any ambiguities. This revision was used to ensure the Qur'an was read aloud without mistakes. Present days, there are two main types of written Arabic:

1. **Qur'anic Arabic** - the language of the Qur'an and Arabic ancient literature. It is different from Classical Arabic mainly in style and vocabulary, some of which is outdated. All Muslims are expected to recite the Qur'an in the original language, however many rely on translations in order to understand the text today. Qur'anic Arabic is considered one of the most complete human languages, rich in vocabulary and complex in its sentence structure.

2. **Classical Arabic** - the universal language of the Arabic-speaking world which is understood by all Arabic speakers. It is the language of the vast majority of written materials, TV shows, journalism and media, etc.

The Qur'anic and Classical Arabic alphabet contains 28 letters. Few additional letters were added to the Classical Arabic to ensure compatibility with other universal languages, especially when writing foreign words containing sounds that do not exist in Arabic, like P or V.

The Arabic language is sometimes called "Loughatou Al Ddaad" which means the language of "Ddaad", referring to a specific letter in the Arabic Alphabet that does not exist in any other languages.

3. ■ How many Arabic dialects do Arabs speak?

Each Arabic speaking country or region has its own variety of spoken dialect. These dialect varieties of Arabic appear in written form in some poetries and documents.

There are 15 types of Arabic dialects approved by historians. All those dialects are a combination of the original local language and Classical Arabic. I asked many Arabs their view about the mixture of Classical Arabic and its variations. They all agreed that the classical Arabic covers at least 70% of the dialect whereas the pronunciation of the words may be different from place to place. That means, a person from Morocco (North West Africa) and Oman (Middle East) have both Arabic as base language but may have some difficulties in communicating with each other. I said difficulties! They still can communicate even though they might have very different accents for the same word.

Through Islam, the Arabic language has spread and expanded over great distances within the time period of less than 1000 years.

Presently, there are six major Classical Arabic dialects as follows:

Egyptian Arabic is spoken by about 80 million people in Egypt. Egyptian Arabic is understood by most Arabs, due to the popularity of Egyptian-made films, video clips and TV shows. Most Arabs agree that Egyptian Arabic dialect sounds very smooth.

Maghrebi Arabic which includes Algerian, Moroccan, Tunisian, Maltese and western Libyan Arabic are also spoken by millions of people across North Africa. The Moroccan and Algerian dialects alone are each spoken by about 20 million people. Maghrebi Arabic is believed to be the most distant from Classical Arabic due to its Berber origins. Some Arab considers Maghrebi Arabic as the roughest of all dialects.

Levantine Arabic dialect includes Syrian, Lebanese, Palestinian, western Jordanian, and countries in the eastern Mediterranean coast. Levantine Arabic is understood by most Arabs because a large part of Lebanese and Palestinian population lives abroad.

Iraqi Arabic has its own flavor due to the Iraqi old civilisations. Iraq is considered the mother of all civilization and this has contributed a lot to the Iraqi Arabic dialect. Americans have been interested in understanding the details of Iraqi dialect for many years and have recruited specialised translators to handle the Iraqi Arabic for their operations.

East Arabian Arabic dialect includes Eastern Saudi Arabia, Eastern Syrian, Jordanian and parts of Oman. This represents a very large geographical area with a very low population.

Gulf Arabic or Khaleeji dialects is spoken in Bahrain, Kuwait, United Arab Emirates, Qatar, and northern Oman. Khaleeji is not a written but a spoken language.

I found traces of two ancient Arabic Dialects considered as dead today. The first one is called Andalusi Arabic, an Arabic dialect spoken in south Spain until 17th century. The second one is called Siculo Arabic, a form of Arabic spoken in Sicily, South Italy until 14th century.

All these dialects are the proof that Arabic language was a major vehicle of culture, especially in science, mathematics and philosophy. In addition to that, many European languages have borrowed many words from Arabic such as the words alcohol and algebra.

4. ■ Why most pan-Arab flags have the same colours?

Before 1918, most of the Arabian Peninsula was invaded by the Turks until the Arab revolt of 1916-1918. Therefore, Arab countries used to have the Ottoman flag for centuries. The Turkish flag use to be red with a moon and a star, and could be seen practically everywhere in the Arabian Peninsula until 1918.

The Arab Revolt was a major time of change in the Arabian Peninsula and Sherif Hussein ibn Ali was the leader of this revolt. Sherif Hussein wanted independence from the Ottoman Turks. Sherif created a single unified Arab state from Aleppo in Syria to Aden in Yemen. Sherif then designed the Arab Revolt flag in June 1916.

Today, Black, Red, White and Green are the Pan-Arab flag colors and have their origins and history plunged deep in the flag of the Arab Revolt. The combination of Black, Red and White are the four colours in the flags of Egypt and Yemen; together with green they are also on the flags of Palestine, Syria, Sudan, Jordan, the United Arab Emirates, Kuwait, and Iraq.

The symbolic origin of these four colours on the pan-Arab flags are:

Black: The messenger of Islam, Prophet Mohammad (570-632 CE)

In pre-Islamic times, the black flag was a sign of revenge. It was the colour of the headband when leading troops into battle. It was during the 7th century in a time that would reflect the continued rise in power of Islam along with the liberation of the beautiful Mecca, that there were two flags – one that was white, as well as one that was black in turn were carried. Inscribed on the white flag were the words, "There is no God but God (Allah) and Mohammad is the Prophet of God". Muslims carried these traditions and both the white and black flags were placed inside the mosque for observation during the Friday prayers. Later on, during what is known as the Abbasid Dynasty (750-1258 CE), rulers of Baghdad, chose the black colour as a symbolic colour in reference to the mourning for the horrific assassination of the relatives of their Prophet Mohammad and it is also in memorandum of the Battle of Karbala. Since then, black is considered to be the colour assigned to Prophet Mohammad.

Red: The Khawarij from Basra, South Iraq (690-730 CE)

The Khawarij were the first Islamic group to appear after the assassination of Caliph Uthman III who was considered by Sunni Muslims as the third of the Four

Rightly Guided Caliphs of Islam. Utman III created the first Republican Party in the early days of Islam using the red flag. Thereafter, Arab tribes who participated in the capture of North Africa and Andalusia also carried the red flag, which became the symbol of the Islamic rulers of Andalusia. The red colour also represents the Hashemites, direct descendants of Prophet Mohammad.

White: For the Umayyad Dynasty from Damascus, Syria (661-750 CE)

The Umayyads Dynasty which ruled for the course of ninety years and they used white for their symbolic colour and is a symbol of the first battle of the Prophet's that occurred at Badr. Umayyads were a major clan of the Quraysh tribe to which Prophet Mohammad belongs. Mu'awia Ibn Abi Sufian (661-750), founded what is known as the Umayyad state and he declared himself as Caliph of Jerusalem. He continued to use the white flag in the holy land for many years.

Green: Symbolizes the Fatimid Dynasty, North Africa (909-1171)

The Fatimids were a Muslim Dynasty that ruled North Africa and some parts of Egypt. The Fatimids were part of the Shiites, claiming to be a descendant of

Fatima, Prophet Mohammad's daughter and her husband Ali, the fourth caliph. They choose green to be their colour, to show an alliance along with loyalty to Ali, who was the cousin of the holy Prophet; he in turn was at one time covered with a green flag instead of the Prophet Mohammad in an attempt to prevent any attempts at assassination.

I heard various other interpretations of these four colours. Some Arabs believe these four colours were chosen as the flag of the Arab revolt for other reasons. Black is for Prophet Mohammad, red for blood, white for peace and green for prosperity.

Regardless of the colour meaning, the Pan-Arab flag shows and demonstrates the Arab unity. I am very impressed by the fact that not only are Arabs unified by the same faith, but they share same language and even the same colours for their flag! We can consider this as Arabs major strength. Throughout this book, we will see that there are many other elements that unify the Arab world, shaping the beauty of Arabia.

5. ■ Why do Arabs greet with "Salam aleikum"?

"Salam aleikum" is the Arabic language greeting used by all Muslim all around the world. It is the most common form of politeness. It is also used at the end of Muslim daily prayers. "Salam aleikum" means "Peace be upon you." and it is done in plural. The religious explanation for this is that Muslims greets both, body and soul. Therefore, the plural form is used to welcome both. The traditional response to "Salam aleikum" is "wa `Alaykum As-Salam". It means "and on you be peace". The word Salam means "Peace" in the Arabic language.

The origin of the Salam greeting is from the Holy book of Qur'an. It is stated that people should say the Salam greeting when entering a house, even if the house is empty. "But when you enter the houses, greet one another with a greeting from Allah say: As-Salaamu 'Alaykum, blessed and good" (Qur'an, Soura al-Noor 24:61)

How do we know to who and when we should say "Salam aleikum"? Several rules and guidelines are available that applies to individuals and groups. These rules were defined by the Holy Prophet. The Prophet Mohammad was asked who should "begin" the Salam greeting, and he replied: "The one who is riding should greet the one who is walking, and the one who is walking should greet the one who is sitting, and the smaller group should greet the larger group."

It is also preferred to use the greeting when arriving and also when leaving. It was reported that Abu Hurayrah, Prophet Mohammad's companion said "When one of you joins a gathering, let him say salaam. When he wants to get up and leave, let him say salaam. The former is not more important than the latter." Abu Hurayrah is considered as one of the most important narrators of the Hadith, a collection of scripts regarded as important tools for determining the Sunnah or Muslim way of life.

In the present day, Muslims around the world use "A.S" or "asa" in their mobile phone text messages (SMS) to carry the greeting. These acronyms of the "Salam Aleikum" are also used in chat-rooms, forums and many other new forms of communications.

In the Middle East, the "Salam" greeting is very common. I have also found the word Salam thousands of miles away from the Middle East and Arab world, used in South East Asia. *Salamat* means "thanks" in Tagalog, the language of the Philippines. Daily Indonesian expressions such as good morning (Selamat Pagi) and welcome (Selamat dating) are from Arabic roots. This is an additional confirmation of the extension of the Arabic language to far horizons.

I see it as one more proof of the Arabic and Islamic unity! At the beginning of the book, I mentioned that in order to understand Arabia, we need to take in consideration many elements that create Arabian unique personality. All these elements are associated and inter-related. All Muslims around the world use the same greetings with the same rules! I am totally fascinated by the fact that Arabs across the Middle East use the same political colours through their pan-Arab unified flags, practically communicate via the same language, share the same faith and even say hello to each other using the same practice!

6. ■ Why do Egyptians speak Arabic and not Egyptian?

We all have been fascinated by the Egyptian civilization and many have wondered why Egyptians speak Arabic instead of Egyptian. Today, Arabic is Egypt's official language. The original Egyptian dialect is now one of the dead languages. Technically, Egyptians might have lost their original Egyptian language, but they have mastered Arabic in their own way. Today, we can confirm that Egyptian Arabic is one of the most understood and recognized Arabic within all Arabic dialects. Egyptians have dominated the Arabic media industry such as television, cinema, radio and music for the last 50 years.

In order to understand why Egyptians speak Arabic, we need to look deep into Egyptian history. Originally, the Egyptian great empire, Pharaoh Era, known as New Kingdom, dominated all its neighbors' countries from 3200 BCE to 1085 BCE. Ancient Egypt's era of pharaohs collapsed when priests took over the Egyptian civilization, and centuries of weakness and chaos followed. Egypt came under consecutive rule from foreign powers, such as the Nubians, the Libyans 712 BCE, the Assyrians 676 BCE and the Persians in 619 BCE.

Immediately after the Persian occupation of Egypt, Alexander the Great conquered Egypt in 323 BCE and a major era of Greek culture began. The Egyptian language was ignored except by some priests and peasants. During the Greek invasion of Egypt, Egyptian was no longer the language of the country, commerce or the language of learning. After the Greeks, the Roman Empire controlled Egypt until 630 CE. This Roman control lasted nearly 700 years and thereafter the Arabs arrived to Egypt.

The Arabs came in at the invitation of the Egyptians (640CE). As for the loss of language, Arabs never enforced Arabic on the Egyptian population. In fact the process of converting to Arabic from a minority language to the language of the majority happened over six centuries. Arabic language was similar to spoken Coptic, the last Egyptian language which is a direct descendant of the ancient Egyptian language written in the hieroglyph. Additionally, Arabic is based on an easy to use alphabet. Therefore, Egyptians started writing their own words using the Arabic alphabets as a sound carrier. The change of language slowly happened as the Egyptian people realized that there are many Arab words that complete their language.

In the modern era of Egypt's history, from 1517 to 1796, Ottoman Turks controlled the entire Egyptian territory. Ottomans were brilliant military strategists and developed a rich Islamic civilization in Egypt. Ottomans used to control Egypt's provinces by relying on the Mamluke army, comprised of Turkish slaves from the Black Sea region. These Turkish slaves had been raised as mercenary soldiers to re-enforce tax collection on Egyptian population. Mamluke is an Arabic word meaning "owned" and truly coincides with the status of the army.

After the Ottoman Turks, the French invaded Egypt in 1798. Egyptians continued to use the Arabic Language as their main verbal and written communication after the Ottoman Turks and French invasions and many years of Christian influence. It is believed that some Egyptian families still teach the French language to their children as they believe it is a superior language. This allows them to differentiate themselves to the masses as upper-class or sophisticates.

Taking into consideration all the foreign control of civilization and history above, Egypt was never ruled by a native Egyptian from the time of Nectanebo II, (343 BCE) until 1952 when Mohammad Naguib came to power. This is equivalent to 2295 years of foreign rulers and amazing cultural blending.

Once more, the Arabic language and Islamic faith combined is proven to be the most effective way of integrating and unifying a civilization such as Egypt. Today, all Egyptians speak and write Arabic and the majority of the country follows the Islamic Faith.

7 ■ Where did the name Egypt come from?

The name of Egypt during ancient times, Pharaoh Era, was Kemet, meaning "Black land", because of the fertile soil of the Nile valley. In some occasions, you might find other names such as "Deshret" which means "Red land." This referred to the desert, which was the dominant landscape of the Egyptian territory.

The name "Egypt" is believed to have come from the original name of Egypt's ancient capital "Hout ka-Ptah" which means "Castle of Ptah.", equivalent to temple of the spirit of God Ptah. At the time, this name was often used even for the country as a whole. I was fascinated to discover that there is a relationship between the word "Hout ka-Ptah" and Egypt! After days of research I realised that the name was shortened and slightly transformed. Considering the original consonants *h-t-k-p-t*, three letters survived into respectively *"k-p-t",* then to be transformed to *"g-p-t."*. This was later translated into the Greek language as 'Ae**gypt**os', and later in English: E**gypt**. The word Copt is an English word taken from ancient Greek work which means Egypt. Therefore the word Copt or Coptic simply means Egyptian referring to the original "Hout ka-Ptah".

In the present, we find that the traditional name for Egypt is now Misr. This beautiful Arabic word means "land" or "fortress" when it is translated. This term is used to refer to the original areas of settlement in Egypt.

When it was first used, the Arab writer's used it to name the city of Cairo. Due to confusion, it now refers to Cairo as well as Egypt as a whole.

Today, the capital of Egypt is Cairo; from the Arabic word Al-Qahira which means "The Victorious". Prior to its creation, the area of Cairo was the site for many cities as it has been renamed many times. The Ancient Egyptian capital was called Memphis (3100 BCE), it was conquered by Persian Empire around 500 BCE and became a fortified settlement. 1100 years later, Arabs took control of Memphis which was at the time controlled by Christian and Jewish nations. The city was then renamed Fustat. Finally, Cairo was established with it's current name in 969 CE by the Fatimids.

Taking in consideration the number of ruling civilizations, cultural blending, and religious mixture, Egypt has a lot to offer. As you noticed, the name Egypt has its Egyptian roots whereas Cairo is from Arabic origin. This is additional evidence that the Arabic culture and language has the power to prevail over the influence of previous civilizations and societies.

8. ■ Are all Arabs Muslims?

The westerns Medias have puzzled all of us with statements such as "Arabs are Muslims". Therefore, most westerns or non-Arab citizens around the world regard Arabs to be Muslims. This statement is generally true but we need to remember that the "Arab World" is expanded from Oman to Morocco covering many countries and ethnicity. The "Muslim World" covers a much larger area including countries in South East Asia, Europe and Southern Africa.

The following statements are also true. Not all Arabs are Muslims, some are Christians or Jewish. Not all Muslims are Arabs or from Arabic origins. As a matter of fact, Iran and Turkey are large Middle Eastern Muslim countries without Arabic origins or roots. Therefore, the simple answer to our question is "No".

Let us overview a few countries considered as Arab but with non Muslim populations such as Egypt, Lebanon, Syria and Jordan.

Today, the largest population of Arabic-speaking Christians is the Copts of Egypt. The word Copt or Coptic simply means Egyptian. We previously discussed the origin of the word. They identify themselves as Egyptians with roots going back to Ancient Egypt. Coptic peoples use the term Arab for people living in the Arabian Peninsula and up until modern times, they have regarded the Arabs as invaders of Egypt. Arabs arrived to Egypt in 640 CE and called the native population of Egypt as Gypt from the Greek word "Aegyptos".

Lebanon contains the largest number of Christians in proportion to its total population. Before the Lebanese Civil War, the Christian Lebanese population was around 45% of the total population. Today, the Lebanese Christians are less than 30% (1,300,000) of the Lebanese population. They belong largely to the Maronite Church, with minorities belonging to the Greek Orthodox and Melkite Greek Catholic church. The Lebanese Maronite community believes in Lebanon's link to the ancient Phoenicians. It is believed that Maronites have a complex ancestry of Greek, Roman, Hebrew, Assyrian and Arab descent all mixed together.

Syria and Jordan population is also mixed with Christian descended Arabs. In Syria there are approximately 10% of Christians. Jordan has a smaller minority of Arab Christian, totaling about 7% of the Jordanian population.

Today, Arab Christians are well integrated in the Arabic Society and have a high level of freedom. Nearly all

Christians belong to the middle or upper classes of the Arab Population.

Finally, Arab Christian population can be considered as an evidence of the multicultural and multi-ethnic foundations of the expanding Arab Muslim world. I hope my explanation has enlightened your view of Arab Muslim and Arab Christians of Arabia.

9

■ Why do Arabs and Jews distrust each other?

Before we cover this sensitive subject, we need to understand the overall environment of the past and present. Firstly, not all Arabs are Muslims and not all Muslims are Arabs. We have already covered this topic previously. While a majority of Arabs are Muslims, there are many non-Muslim Arabs around the world. Secondly it is important to remember that not all Arabs dislike Jews, that not all Muslims dislike Jews, and that not all Jews dislike Arabs and Muslims. To avoid stereotyping people, I have been looking to the origin of Arabs/Jews distrust and the contemporary issues between these two communities. I have carefully used the word "distrust" and avoid the word "dislike'. The following answer is a mixture of history, religious facts and common sense.

Apparently, the historical facts can be traced back to Prophet Abraham and his descendants. It is believed that Jews are descendants of Abraham's son Isaac whereas the Arabs are descendants of Abraham's son Ishmael. This is very simplified view of the history but that is what people remember!

Jewish main scripts of faith such as Genesis, the Tanakh and the Old Testament have many chapters regarding the mistrust and contempt of the two brothers, Isaac and Ishmael, towards each other. Genesis means the Beginning or

Origin and is considered as "The First Book of Moses". The Hebrew Scriptures confirm that the promised son of Abraham was Isaac.

On the other hand, the holy Qur'an contains very clear instructions for Muslims regarding Jews. Muslims are instructed to treat Jews as brothers and in the other hand are commanded to convert all Jews to Islam. Additionally, the Qur'an confirms that Ishmael is Abraham's promised son and was almost sacrificed to the Lord (in contradiction to Genesis chapter 22). I believe, this debate over who was the son of promise contributes in some shape and form to the distrust today.

However, the ancient root of bitterness between Isaac and Ishmael does not explain all of the distrust between Jews and Arabs today. In fact, for thousands of years of Middle Eastern history, Jews and Arabs lived in relative peace and indifference toward each other.

It is suggested that the distrust between Arabs and Jews has a more modern origin. After World War II, the United Nations provided a portion of the land of Palestine to the International Jewish community which was at that time mainly inhabited by the Palestinians. At the time, most Arabs protested against the nation of Israel occupying the land. Regardless of much opposition, the State of Israel was created. Two years after the end of the Second World War, the first Arab-Israeli War started in 1948. This war is also known as the Israeli War of Independence and was the first in a series of wars between Israel and Arabic neighboring countries in the long-running Arab-Israeli conflict.

This war was the beginning of Palestinian Arabs "al Nakba", which means "the Catastrophe" in Arabic. For Israelis, the war marked the successful establishment of the Israeli state. Ever since, there has been great hostility between Israel and it's Arab neighbor countries. The Israeli / Palestinian issue is currently a daily subject on most TV channels and newspapers throughout the world.

Today, the Jew and Arab distrust is a political subject, not a religious one. Muslims have no historical grievance against Jews and did not engage in periodic massacres like those that happened repeatedly in Europe, causing many Jews to flee south.

After sixty years of war between Palestine and Israel, there is now what I call the Arab rejection of Jewish mentality and political ideology which is leading to a Palestinian genocide. Therefore, most Islamic countries ban or despise the Jewish state.

Until February 2004, the official website for the Saudi Arabia Supreme Commission for Tourism announced it would deny any Jewish person a Visa for the country. Outraged by this incident, the US Government threatened to decline visas to any Saudi nationals unless the Saudi government reversed that ruling against religious parties. In agreement the Saudi government chose to change the wording of the disputed statement. In the present time, some areas prohibit the use of Israeli passports that have arrival and departure stamps on them, including Israeli citizens.

We all hope for a brighter future for the Palestinian citizens and look forward to a sustainable peace treaty between Israel and Palestine. I personally believe a total removal of all military weapons and arms from both countries should be the starting point, which would demonstrate that both countries are willing to live in peace.

10. ■ Why Al-Cohol sounds like it is from Arabic origin?

The *al–* in *alcohol* is a word that has its origins deep inside the Arabic language, as is the case with *algebra* and *alkali*. *Al-* is the Arabic word corresponding to *"the"* in English.

Today we use the word Alcohol for drinks or chemical substance used in Medicine. Drinking Alcohol probably reminds you of wine, beer or contemporary drinks such as Vodka. Alcohol can also remind you of the colorless bottle of liquid that we find in hospitals and clinics, used for sterilization of wounds and supplies.

The word Alcohol isn't what it used to be. The Arabic ancestor of Cohol was *kuḥl,* a fine powder made from antimony sulfide and used by women as a cosmetic powder around the eyes 2500 years ago. Arabs used alcohol as a cosmetic product way before the rest of the world. In Yemen, they used to blow the powder directly into their eyes to increase sparkle. Other women used it as a paste and rubbed it on the eyelids. The Kuhl powder is so refined that a person couldn't feel the separate grains when they were rubbed between the fingers. By the 1st century CE, Egyptians, Greeks, Romans culture were already using Kuhl as makeup to enhance womanhood.

Later on, Arabian alchemists invented the distillation of alcohol around 1,000 CE. The English word *alcohol,* got its origins through Latin from Arabic. The first time the word Alcohol was used in Europe was in 1543. Arabic chemists used *al-kuḥl* to refer to other substances that were obtained by distillation. By the time "alcohol" entered English dictionary in 1672, its meaning was changed and included all distilled drinks. In 1753, liquid spirits, the new form of Alcoholic drinks were also called Alcohol or spirits.

This was the transformation of the original Arabic word Kuhl to the modern times Alcohol. As you already know, drinking Alcohol is forbidden for all Muslims around the world. We will look into its origin in the next question; why do people clink their glasses together before drinking alcohol? I traced the answer back to medieval times. It was very common to kill someone by poisoning their drink. Therefore, in order to trust each other, the host would clink their wine or beer glass strongly with their guests. The little exchange of liquid between the two glasses demonstrated the fact that the offered drink is poison free. Today, this very old gesture represents trust, honesty and toast to good health.

11. ■ Why is alcohol forbidden in Islam?

We all know that alcohol is a forbidden consumable within Islam. It is what Muslims consider as an "intoxicant", derived from the Greek word Tox, which means poison. If you look closely to the word Tox, you will find derivatives such as Toxin, which means a poison carrier.

"Intoxicants" are forbidden in the Qur'an through several separate verses. First of all, Qur'an forbids Muslims to attend to prayers while intoxicated (Soura 4:43). Then a later verse says that alcohol contains some good and some evil, but the evil is greater than the good (Soura 2:219). This was part of the process in turning people away from consuming the alcohol. Finally, Qur'an clearly mentions that "intoxicants and games of chance" are "abominations of Satan's handiwork," (Soura 5:90-91).

It also remains true that the Qur'an is out of chronological order. This means that some of the later verses of this holy book were not revealed after their previous counter parts.

In the first verse cited above, the word for "intoxicated" is *sukara* which means Sugar in Arabic. In this context, it means drunk or intoxicated. Soura 4:43 doesn't mention the alcoholic drink but simply refers to intoxication. In the next verses cited, the word which is often translated as "wine" or "intoxicants" is *al-khamr*, which is related to the verb "to ferment." This word could be used to describe other intoxicants such as beer or wine.

Muslims interpret these Qur'anic verses in total to forbid any intoxicating substance including beer, wine, and spirits such as Vodka, Arak or any alcoholic products or drinks currently available on the market. It is important to understand that there is not a ban in the Qur'an on alcohol because it is an intoxicant. The reason for the banning is because it will make the good Muslim forget their prayers and God, and that is far more harmful than anything else.

It is written that Prophet Mohammad instructed his followers, at the time, to avoid any intoxicating substances, "If it intoxicates in a large amount, it is forbidden even in a small amount." For this reason, most Muslims avoid alcohol; even small amounts used in cooking.

Arabic foods and drinks are totally alcohol free. Therefore, if you are a non Muslim and invite your Muslim friends for lunch or dinner, it would be polite to respect their rules. If any alcohol has been used to cook or prepare the dishes, warn your guest as a sign of respect.

12. ■ What is the Arak ?

The word Arak comes from Arabic origins and means "sweet" or "juice". Eastern Mediterranean Arab populations call it the "milk of lions". Arak is considered the grand grand-father of today's modern alcoholic drinks. Arak, sometimes also spelt "Araq", is a clear, colourless and unsweetened drink with strong anise flavor. Arak is mostly produced in the Eastern Mediterranean and is the national alcoholic drink of Lebanon, Syria, Jordan, Palestine and Iraq.

Arak is usually mixed in approximately 1/3 Arak to 2/3 water and ice is then added. Once you do this, it causes the Arak to turn to an opaque milky-white colour. Sometimes people mix Arak with teas and juices. It is very important to add the water before the ice. This is to avoid the creation of an unpleasant skin on the surface of the drink due to the chemical reaction. For this reason, an Arak glass is never refilled twice. Instead a clean glass is used each time. The alcoholic strength of the Arak depends on its quality, origin and distillation technique and varies usually between 30% and 60%.

Under the eyes of the Christian minorities, Arak was developed out in the Islamic region. During this early Islamic era, Jabir ibn Hayyan invented the alembic which is a simple distillation equipment. Its official name in Lebanon is Al Karkeh or sometimes Al Kattara. However, Muslims did not use Jabir's invention to produce alcoholic beverages since, in Islam; the consumption of alcohol is not permitted. They used the discovery to produce perfume from flowers and to produce kuhl, the woman's cosmetic powder.

Arabs carried the art of distilling kuhl to Spain from where it reached the rest of Europe. In these Christian lands, the distillation techniques were used thereafter to produce alcoholic drinks of all kinds.

Traditionally, Arak was only available from local or village producers, but in the last century it has been industrialized. There are many large manufacturing plants especially in Lebanon. Until this day, Arak is a very popular alcoholic drink in the Middle East, in competition with the many drinks imported from the West.

While Arak is extremely popular in Syria, the most esteemed brands are Lebanese such as Ksara and Massaya. Iraqi Arak, which is less known, is matching the Lebanese quality and it is made out of dates instead of Anise. Many Lebanese and Iraqi drinkers distil their own Arak liquor. The quality of home-made Arak called "Arak Baladi" is considered superior to commercial brands. In some restaurants you might be served home-made Arak at a very high price. Many Lebanese towns are famous for their high quality home-made Arak production such as Zahle in the Bekaa valley or Toula, a village in the Northern Lebanese Mountains.

As you noticed, Arak is mainly used in western part of Arabia. The population of the central Middle East does not use Arak at all as they strictly follow Islamic traditions.

13. ■ What is a halal meal?

Halal is an Arabic word which means allowed or permitted. The opposite of Halal in Arabic is Haram, which means illegal or prohibited. Halal and Haram are universal Islamic concepts that apply to all facets of Islamic life.

While many things are clearly Halal or clearly Haram, there are some things which are not clear at all. There are some items which tend to be considered questionable, because we need more information to classify them. These items of question are referred to as Mashbooh, which means doubtful or questionable. Foods containing ingredients such as gelatin, enzymes, and emulsifiers are questionable (Mashbooh) because the origin of these ingredients is not known.

In order to make the meat Halal, it must be properly slaughtered by a Muslim or by what we call "the People of the Book" such as Christians (Qu'ran verse 5:5), while mentioning the name of God (Allah in Arabic). The proper Islamic method of slaughtering an animal is called Dhabiha. During the Dhabiha, the animal may not be killed by being boiled or electrocuted, and the carcass should be hung upside down long enough to be blood-free. It is proven scientifically that blood free meat is healthier than others.

Different rules apply to fish and in general, fish with scales are always Halal. Some Islamic jurisprudences (Islam specialists) declare shellfish and scale-less fish such as catfish to be Haram. This is subject to debate in some Arabic countries.

Items that receive the classification of Halal, is a matter which is taken very seriously in the Muslim world. It can only be carried out by someone that understands the Islamic Dietary laws.

Islamic dietary laws began long ago, in the Qur'an, dictated to the Prophet Mohammad by the Angel Gabriel around 620 AD. There are two other sources of information about Islamic Dietary laws. The first one is the "Sunnah", the actions of the Prophet, or the things he recommended or approved. The second source of information is the "hadith" which are ancient Islamic scripts determining Muslim way of life, the sayings of the Prophet, relayed through people who knew him. The combination of all three sources of information makes up the rules of Islam and therefore Islamic Dietary Laws. There is no centralized Islamic authority, so there are differences of opinion based on the Shariah considered as religious legislation, varying by region or country.

For westerners, there are some simple rules to follow: generally, all foods are considered halal except the following, which are haram:

- Pork and it's by-products
- Animals improperly slaughtered or dead before slaughtering
- Animals killed in the name of anyone other than Allah
- Alcohol and intoxicants
- Carnivorous animals (Animals eating meat such as lions or tigers), birds of prey and land animals without external ears
- Blood and blood by-products
- Any foods contaminated by or prepared with any of the above products

Many western fast food chains have adjusted their food production line in accordance with the Islamic rules and beliefs. You can commonly find in many Arabic countries Halal burgers or other Halal international dishes. The word Halal is sometimes viewed as a trusted source and some Muslims may simply purchase the goods without questioning. In some occasions, advertisement agencies and marketing specialists misuse the Halal concept to sell irrelevant products to Muslim consumers.

In some countries such as United Arab Emirates, many shopping centres keep Haram goods and all pork related products in separate sections of shopping centres in order to attract foreign customers. The Haram food chain products are always handled by non-Muslim workers usually from the Philippines or India. United Arab Emirates policy towards Haram food is very clear and many food specifications exist within the health ministry to control such goods.

This is one more proof that Islamic beliefs are open to diversity and acceptance of other religions or traditions.

14. ■ Where does Kebab come from?

Kebab is a very popular Arabian food, it is certain that you will find the kebab on any Arabic restaurant menu. Kebab is so popular that there are many sorts of them and there are even different specialties and versions per country.

Food historians generally agree that the origin of kebabs goes back to ancient Middle Eastern cooks. In areas where the material to create a fire would be difficult to fine, this provided a new and conservative way of cooking meat. Small pieces of meat threaded on skewers required less fire and a shorter cooking time, in other words, smaller the cut, faster the cooking time. The recipes and combinations are as endless as Arabia is wide.

The word Kebab is from Persian origin and means less (Kamb) water (Aab). Originally, it meant fried meat instead of grilled meat. Kebab is mentioned in a 14th century dictionary as a "Tabahajah", a Persian name for a dish of fried meat pieces.

While in the English language, the term kebab remains to the traditional shish kebab, in its current meaning, it keeps its Turkish origin.

Originally this dish was given to the Turkish soldiers of medieval times who would eat their meat skewered on their battle swords. While others contest that this dish has been around far longer than those times. But whatever the true origins and facts, it is indisputable that kabab cooking provides a quality dish with a great taste.

Supporting the later claim, there are pictures of Byzantine Greeks who are making dishes that appear to be similar to the shish kebabs. Perhaps this has something to do with the fact that even in those times, methods to keep fires alive were so limited.

Ibn Battuta (1304-1377 CE), a pioneer Arab traveler and explorer of the Islamic World, records that shish kebab was served in the royal houses of India, possibly predating the Sultanate period, and even commoners would enjoy it for breakfast with bread called "naan".

In Andalusia, a variant of the shish kebab, known as *Pinchos Morunos* or Moorish sticks, is very prominent, and is usually eaten during summer barbecues. These are usually made of Pork or Chicken meat.

The Turkish term, *Döner kebab*, is a form of slow roasting lamb or chicken on a vertical spit. This meat then closely resembles what you would find in the gyro. Döner kebab is popularly served in pita bread, as it is best known, with salad. It is also served in a dish with a salad and bread or French fries on the side, or used for Turkish pizzas called "pide" or "kebabpizza". Take-out döner kebab or shawarma restaurants are common in many parts of Europe. Döner kebab is said to be a best-selling fast food in Germany, Poland and Romania as well as being very popular in the UK, France, The Netherlands, Norway, Denmark, Sweden, Finland, Italy, Canada, Ireland and Australia. Take-out gyros are popular in the United States, where beef and lamb are typically used; shawarma is mostly available in ethnic neighborhoods, but döner kebab is relatively unknown outside of large cities like New York City.

In the UK kebabs are most popularly eaten as a meal after a night out, and many kebab shops will do their main business in the hours after the local pubs and clubs have closed. The same applies for The Netherlands, Ireland, Australia and Scandinavia.

15. ■ Why do Arabs offer coffee instead of tea?

Coffee or Khahwa is not just a drink, especially among the Bedouins and Gulf countries societies. Tea is the everyday drink whereas coffee is a ceremony for visitors and guests. Arabs consider drinking coffee together as a symbol of harmony and trust. If you live in the Arabian Gulf, your business partner will offer you Arabic Coffee served during the meetings. I suggest you welcome your Arab friends by preparing Khahwa using the following technique:

To make traditional Arabic coffee, Khahwa, you will need to start with green coffee beans and some cardamom seeds. The Arabic coffee is composed of about one part coffee beans, to three parts of water, and half a part of cardamom. Place the coffee beans in a dry frying pan and toast the beans until the color turns to golden brown then cool them down. Put the cardamom seeds in a grinder and make sure they are ground to a fine powder. Go back to the cooling coffee beans and remove the flakes. Grind the beans so they are still fairly coarse. Mix the ground coffee with the cardamom in a pot, and add hot water. Then boil the drink so that it starts to foam. Pour this into a serving pot and you are ready to serve it immediately. Do not add any milk or sugar to Arabic coffee. We can consider the Khahwa the equivalent of western Expresso.

As the khahwa is served in porcelain cups that have no handles, the tradition of serving the Arabic coffee has begun. While the host begins to serve his guests he places a stack of cups into his right hand, while leaving the coffee pot on the left. At this time, he will pour a small taste of the black liquid and take a sample to show everyone it is suitable for drinking. After determining so, he pours coffee for the primary guest then serves the other guests. After each guest is served, he pours a cup for himself and joins them.

From my experience, the cup will not be full and it may only contain a little bit of coffee allowing you to consume it in a couple of sips. This coffee is typically served unsweetened to maintain the bitter taste. It is used as a symbol in reference to how harsh the desert can be.

Traditionally, the guest will be offered at least three cups of coffee as each cup has specific significance. With the first cup served, which is called, "Finhan al dayf" the host is welcoming their guest and a mutual trust is shown. This first cup is followed by a second cup called, "Finjan al sayf", this means "the Sword cup". With this second cup, both men honor that they will resolve any conflicts that may be between the two of them. The final cup, "finjan al kayf" is to be enjoyed as a pleasure cup and used to continue enjoyment and conversation.

I noticed that on some occasions, the significance of the three cups simply means health, love and future generations. It is very rude not to drink all three rounds as it means you have bad intentions. I suggest you to use your right hand to drink and eat at all times. More rounds and refills may well be offered, and you are free to drink as much as you want. Be aware that Arabic coffee is considered as a luxury and it is usually followed by tea.

Finally, throwing the coffee into the fire has many meanings in the Arab world. It is believed that throwing coffee in the fire is the beginning of bad luck and in some occasions it will release the demons. Additionally, do not spit out the coffee if you don't like the taste as it means that you dishonor the host.

Once again, a simple cup of coffee, filled with traditions, is the perfect example of Arabian hospitality. You will find very similar hospitality from Oman to Morocco with the same cup of Coffee and similar taste. I believe this is beyond any Arabic national traditions proving that Arabs have truly mastered the capacity of sharing well-mannered traditions beyond the boundaries of the Arabian Peninsula.

16. ■ Why is the Oryx a sign of many Arabic countries?

There are various types of Oryx in the Middle East and North Africa. Gemsbok Oryx in the Kalahari Desert and scimitar-horned Oryx in the Sahara and the Beisa of the East African Somali desert are very well known. Apparently, the most praised Oryx is the Arabian one, the desert specialist. With a curved set of horns, it might be the actual origin of the unicorn. In profile, the two long horns appear as one, which may be the origin of legendary sightings of Unicorns. The Arabian Oryx's colour is a white coat which helps to reflect the hot desert sun. During winter, the Oryx's coat changes to a darker colour and its hairs will stand erect to absorb the sun's warmth.

Historically, Oryx's live in groups of 2 to 15; traveling through Arabia and the Gulf States, up through Jordan and into Syria and Iraq. Before 1940's, Bedouins used to hunt the Arabian Oryx on their Camels using simple rifles or guns. From 1945, they started to use heavy hunting and automatic weapons which resulted in a severe reduction in the number of Arabian Oryx population. The illegal hunts continued and in 1972 the Arabian Oryx was virtually distinct, with the exception of a few private collections in Arabia, including the United Arab Emirates and the World Herd in the USA.

There are various projects to repopulate the Oryx across Arabia. The most famous project was initiated by the United Arab Emirates' late president, His Highness Sheikh Zayed bin Sultan Nayhan on the Baniyas Island, off the coast of Abu Dhabi. This particular project did boost the number of Arabian Oryx's and provided some major research opportunities. This is part of a conservation of heritage program deployed by the royal family few decades ago.

In the early Islamic era, a famous Arabic poet, Umar ibn Abi Rabi'ah wrote: "Graceful as an Oryx they brought her out, slowly walking between five budding beauties". For centuries, Arab poets wrote about the Arabian Oryx. In most cases in these poems, the Oryx wins against the hunter and his dogs.

Since it will never run from a battle, The Oryx is the designated symbol of dignity, pride and power. No matter if it won or lost the Oryx would remain fighting its attacker.

This is why almost all Arab poems ended with the Oryx triumphing over man's own hunting dogs. For this particular reason, Oryx is represented in some Arab countries flags, emblems and artifacts. Today, Oryx is the national animal and the symbol of Qatar.

17. ■ Why do Arabs hunt with Falcons?

For thousands of years, falconry was regarded as a noble and artistic part of desert life. Originally, falcons were used for hunting by the Bedouins and nomads in the Arabian Peninsula. Falcons were used to hunt the Hare or Houbara Bustard, birds living in the Arabian Peninsula and prized by the Bedouins for their taste.

We can trace falcon hunting back to 2500 years ago. The falconer was seen as a figure of authority and power. When depicted in pictures, you will normally see a falconer on horseback along with his companions as a falcon is posed to land on his hand. As the falconer controlled his falcon, so he controlled his territory. This image and posture is still used in the Arab world. I have personally seen such images in United Arab Emirates such as with the late president, His Highness Sheikh Zayed bin Sultan Nayhan, seated on a white horse with a falcon on his arms.

Today, falconry is a sport and no longer a way of life. The Arabian Peninsula is the only place in the world where falconry is still an important sporting activity. There are several other falconry clubs in Europe and United States, but the Gulf States have taken this sport to the highest levels. In February

2003, one of the most remarkable events in the recorded history of falconry took place when a falcon owned by Sheikh Mohammad from the United Arab Emirates brought down a deer many times its own weight during a long and difficult fight. The people of the Gulf have a strong personal commitment to falconry and ensure that it is practiced in the correct manner, with the proper respect due to Islamic customs. The United Arab Emirates emblem (Symbol) is an open wing falcon which represents all seven Emirates as one. The falcon represents power, purity and independence.

Generally, there are two types of Falcons, the farm falcon and the wild falcon. It is reported by Bedouins that the wild falcon is highly sensible hunter and is capable in some occasions to see the prey from long distances of up to 1.5 Km and instinctively hunt it down. Falcon's eyes are obviously more accurate and receptive than the human eye. The hunter simply needs to elevate the falcon in the air and the bird will immediately spot any prey in the area. Farm falcons are also very sensible hunters but in many occasions, they are distracted by other birds or objects when hunting.

In the UAE and some GCC countries, each falcon has a microchip inserted beneath its skin as an aid to future identification. Some very expensive falcons are fitted with miniature satellite transmitters so that their movements can be tracked anywhere in the world. The microchip and satellite trackers simplify the process of identification and ownership between Bedouins.

The two main species of falcon kept in the UAE are the Saker and the Peregrine. The Peregrine falcon has dark tone colour, brown-and-cream plumage, and can fly at high speed sometimes over 200km/h, making it the fastest of all living creatures. For this particular reason, the falcon has been used as a domesticated hunter by Bedouins and nomads. It is believed that wild falcons always have a greater sense of hunting than farm grown falcons.

The trapping and training of falcons requires special skills, a lot of patience and bravery. Once a falcon is captured, the falconer starts educating and training it. The trainers usually cover the falcon's eyes with a leather hood and they deprive it of food in order to make it easier to educate. Usually, in the first few weeks of falcon training, the falconer stays with the falcon at all times to create a close relationship with the bird. Then the falcons are then put through a various exercise programs to complete their training. Once trained, the falcon can hold a captured Houbara Bustard without killing it. This way, the Bedouin can kill the prey with Islamic traditions making it Halal.

18. ■ Why are Arabian horses considered the best?

Arabian horses have a long history. There is archaeological evidence of horses that resemble modern Arabian horses, dating back 4,500 years.

A few hundred years ago, in the deserts of the Middle East, a Middle Eastern breed of horse was recognized and since then influenced the world. It all started somewhere along the Euphrates and Tigris Rivers in the countries that are now known as Syria and Iraq. This horse breed developed and became known as the Arabian horse.

First of all we need to understand the Arabian horse's physical traits. The Arabian horse has distinctive physical structure as compared to other breeds. The first noticeable distinction is the fact that the Arabian horse is smaller than other horses. The Arabian horse's colour can vary between chestnut, grey, brown, and black. White markings on the face and legs are common. The Arabian horse has many other characteristics such as a beautiful and delicate head, large eyes, a high-set, arched neck and a high tail carriage. The Arabian horse body structure is defined by muscular legs, broad strong joints, large shoulders and a muscular chest. Arabian horse specialists have many more specific details to describe these horses. I simply described the most visible characteristics. In my opinion, for most of us, non-experts, the easiest way to recognize an Arabia horse is its small size and very large nasals. As they run fast, they need more air than other horses. All these physical characteristics combined with their strength, speed and intelligence make the Arabian horse the best horse in the world.

Secondly, we need to understand the religious beliefs and traditions surrounding the Arabian horses. The original Arabs and Bedouins living in the Arabian Peninsula considered this breed of horse as a gift from Allah. Many beliefs are related to the Arabian horses. This is why Arabs respect and value these horses more than any other belongings. It was believed that the bulging forehead called Jibbah was a sign of the blessings of Allah. So, the greater the "Jibbah" the greater the blessings carried by the horse. It was also believed that the great arching neck with a high crest, the "Mitbah" was a sign of courage. As the Arabs had a very high esteem for these traits, the Arabian horses' selective breeding was focused to enhance these characteristics. Any mixture of foreign blood from the mountains or the cities surrounding the desert was strictly forbidden. We can confirm that religious belief, superstition and tradition influenced the Arabian horse breeding.

Third, we need to understand the role of the Arabian horses in the daily Arabic life. Centuries ago, the leaders of the tribes use to pass from generation to generation stories and legends about their family horses. As part of daily life and Arabian culture, they used to have horse racing with primitive rules. Horse race winners took the best of the loser's herd as their prize.

Breeding stock could be bought and sold; in other words it was a commercial transaction. Today, if an Arabian horse is given as a gift, it is considered as the most honored gift of all. No greater offering could be given than an Arabian horse.

Today, many Middle Eastern countries rulers and Sheikhs continue to breed Arabian Horses at these high standards, especially in the Gulf region. The prices of specific Arabian horses can reach millions of dollars. United Arab Emirates, particularly Dubai, is considered the richest horse racing area in the world, attracting millions of fans and the best horses in the world.

19. Why is the Qur'an considered a mathematical wonder?

Galileo once said, "*Mathematics is the language with which God has written the universe*". This may actually be interpreted as quite a true statement once you read about the mathematical wonders of the Qur'an.

The Qur'an is characterized by a unique phenomenon that is not found in any other human composed book. Every element of the Qur'an is composed with some mathematical purpose, and it appears that number 19 is the key to Qur'an's structure. Many mathematical evaluations of the text, including that by non Muslim researchers, have concluded that number 19 is the key element of Qur'an mystery. Numerous works of literature have been published that point to the various scientific miracles and mysteries of the Qur'an.

There are two major facets of the Quran's mathematical system: Firstly, the mathematical structure involving the numbers of souras and verses or words, and secondly the mathematical literary composition. Skeptics might say the following are coincidences, but I believe there is an element of supernatural or Divine purpose in the following facts:

- Both the words Al-Rajl (Man) and Al-Mara'a (Woman) are mentioned 24 times each in the Qur'an

- The word *Al-Shahr* (Month in English) is mentioned 12 times.

- The word *Al-Yahom* (Day in English) is mentioned 365 times.

- Both the words *Al-Hayat* (Life) and *Al-Maout* (death) are mentioned 145 times each in the Qur'an.

- Both the words *Devil* and *Angel* are mentioned 88 times each.

- There are many other mathematical balances with other subjects in Qur'an that might prove the Mathematical structure of the Holy book.

The Mathematical composition in it's literary sense is a more complex subject. Simplified and clarified, I can explain the literary composition of the Qur'an based on the facts of number 19. Chapter 74 of the Qur'an, God's Final Testament, is dedicated to the number 19. The name of that chapter is "Al-Muddassir" which means "The Hidden Secret". The number 19 is specifically mentioned in that Chapter as a punishment for those who state that the scripture is human-made (Soura 74:25), and proclaims that the number 19 is "One of the greatest" (Soura 74:35). The implications of this number as proof for the authenticity of the Qur'an remained unknown for centuries. There are some additional facts that point out the number 19 as extraordinary number, and it's presence throughout the Qur'an is quite impressive.

- The first verse (1:1), known as "Basmalah," consists of 19 letters.

- The Qur'an consists of 114 souras, which is 19 x 6.

- The total number of verses in the Qur'an is 6346 equal to 19 x 334.

- The addition of the digit of the number of souras can be simplified and reduced to the number 19, (6346) is 6+3+4+6 =19.

- The last revelation (Soura 110) consists of 19 words.

- The first verse of the last revelation (110:1) consists of 19 letters.

Coincidence or a true revelation, we have to consider that the Holy Book was written in an extraordinary manner. Additionally, taking into consideration that each word of Qur'an was recited by Prophet Mohammad's followers, word for word in order to keep the content intact.

Over time, there will be more research and more wonders discovered through the Qur'an. Some people believe that the mathematical formulas hidden within the Qur'an represent the key answers to the nature of God.

20. Why Arabic names are mostly without a surname?

We have all encountered very complex Arab names and once translated from Arabic to English, we can get many varieties of the same name. For example Muhamad, Mohammed and Mohamad are all the same in Arabic but once transcribed in English, they are written differently.

Old Arabic names are based on a long naming system: most Arabs do not simply have first/middle/last names, but a full chain of names which are used throughout the Arab world. This is an issue in our modern computer world which is designed for first/middle/surname only. Also, I noticed that the most common names in the Middle East and Arab world are Ahmed and Mohammad. This can be also a problem in many computer systems. When you search for any of these names, there are too many of them and it makes the search very difficult. Ahmed in Arabic means "Worthy of Praise" and Mohammad means "The praised one".

Due to the importance of the Arabic language in Islam, a large majority of Muslims use Arabic naming convention. This naming convention might look complicated for Europeans and other cultures, but they are seamless in the Arab world.

The naming convention is divided into five distinctive parts that makes up a person's name.

1. Ism
2. Kunya
3. Nasab
4. Laqab
5. Nisba

Ism is the main name of an Arab person, his or her personal name such as "Khaled" or "Manal". Most Arabic names are originally Arabic words with a meaning, usually about the good character of the person.

The Kunya precedes the Ism when not replacing it. Kunya is the person's first-born child and in some cases replace the Ism. For example, "Abu Ali" for "Father of Ali". The female variant of Abu is "Umm", like "Umm Ali".

The Nasab provide details of the person's legacy by the word ibn which means "son". In some occasion ibn can be pronounced Bin. Therefore, Ibn Khaled means "son of Khaled". Sometimes, many nasab can follow each other and trace a person's ancestry backwards in time. This was important in the tribal societies of the ancient Arabs. The nasab is a form of identification and a social and political status within the tribe.

The laqab is the description of the person. Laqab is not commonly used in the Middle East. It is considered as an old way of naming.

Finally, the nisba describes the person's profession or location or family descent. Nisba is the equivalent of the Western surname. It will follow an entire family through generations. As an example, Al-Filastini means from Palestine.

Let's review the above with few real examples: "Abu Ali Mohammad al-Jamil ibn Nidal ibn Abdulaziz al-Filastini" which means "Father-of-Ali, Mohammad, who is the beautiful, son of Nidal, who is the son of Abdulaziz, the Palestinian".

If a man's name is "Saleh bin Tariq bin Khalid Al-Mansouri", "Saleh" is his personal name and is the name that his family and friends would call him by. "Bin" translates as "son of", so "Tariq" is Saleh's father's name. "Bin Khaled" means that Tariq was the son of Khalid, making Khalid the grandfather of Saleh. "Al-mansouri" would be Saleh's family name. So "Saleh bin Tariq bin Khalid Al-Mansouri" translates as "Saleh, son of Tariq, son of Khaled; of the family Al-Mansouri."

I suppose you have a smile on your face by now and you are probably scratching your head wondering why Arabs have such complex names. This naming convention was designed for tribal life in combination with the Arabic language. English translation of Arab names adds an extra layer of complexity to it. Simply imagine these names written in a European passport. Most embassies around the world would like to comply with the westerns standards of first name, middle name and surname and are currently facing difficulties with Arab naming standards.

In conclusion, the Arabic naming convention is different that the international standards. I believe Arabs put in a lot of effort to simplify this convention to be able to comply with international naming rules. The beauty of the Arabic naming convention is that you can be called in many different ways. Your name involves the name of your parents, your root origin, your close family name…etc. On many occasions, I noticed that the different part of an Arabic name is used depending on the situation. This is just another example of the flexibility, complexity, and diversity of the Arabic culture alive in the Middle East.

21.■Why Muslim man can marry more than once?

I am sure you have already came across the word Polygamy. Many people believe that Islam allows Polygamy. Obviously, this is not a correct statement. Polygamy means a system of marriage whereby one person has more than one spouse regardless of being a man or woman. The term polygamy (poly: Many gamy: Marriage) comes from ancient Greek. There are two type of Polygamy, polygyny and polyandry.

Polygyny is when a man has more than one wife at the same time. This is the most common form of polygamy. Polyandry is the specific form of polygamy in which a woman is married to more than one husband in the same time. In Islam, limited polygyny, up to four wives, is allowed and polyandry is completely forbidden.

I searched for the exact Soura that specifies the rules of polygamy in Islam and I found the following statement. Allah says in the Holy Qur'an: "Marry women of your choice, two, or three, or four; but if you fear that you shall not be able to deal justly (with them), then only one." (Soura 4:3)

Before the Qur'an's clear regulation of polygamy, there was no limit for polygyny within the Arabian Peninsula and many men had many wives, some even hundreds. Islam has limited the polygyny to four wives. In the Qur'an, it is clearly mentioned that the husband should be fair with all his wives and treat them equally. For example, he has to provide separate living accommodations for each of his wives. There are many stories about Polygyny in the Middle East. One man had 11 wives and when he converted to Islam, he asked Prophet Mohammad: "What should I do with my wives?" Prophet Mohammad replied: "Divorce them all except four."

Therefore polygyny is not a rule or an order but an exception. Many non-Muslim people are under the misconception that it is obligatory for all Muslim man to have more than one wife. Very few Muslim colleagues and friends of mine have more than one wife.

The reason for multiple wives in Islam was not to satisfy men's desires but for the well being of the widows and the orphans of the wars. During war times, many women were unable to find husband's and they preferred to be a co-wife than no wife. Additionally, in the Arabian Peninsula the family continuity depends on sons. Sons carry the name of the family whereas daughters lose their name to other families. In some cases, women cannot hold property and so a male child can retain family wealth. Therefore, allowing multiple marriages is useful to make sure that there will be a son in the family. In the Arabian Peninsula, a man can't marry another woman without the knowledge of his wife. He should tell her, for she might refuse such situation and in this case it is totally her right if she asked for divorce.

Prophet Mohammad was a very good example and he followed the rules of Qur'an. Prophet Mohammad was married to only one woman, Khadijah. He stayed devoted to her from age 24 to 50. Only after her death did Prophet Mohammad remarry again.

Islam has several other marriage rules such as: Muslim men can marry non-Muslim women, yet Muslim woman are prohibited from marring a non-Muslim man. This has ensured the spread of Islam through marriage and continuous family growth.

In conclusion, the Arabic world combined with Islam marriage regulations allows Islam to spread across all corners of the planet. The Islamic marriage regulatory authority is now the Shariah Law which is the mandatory Law of Union in the Islamic world.

22. ■ Why do Arab women use henna on their body?

Centuries of migration and cultural interaction make it very difficult to locate the origin of Henna. Historians argue that henna has been used for at least 3500 years in both cosmetic and healing capacities. Some historians argue that henna was invented in ancient India while others claim it was brought to India by Egyptians. There are some indications that the tradition of applying henna to the female body started in the Middle East.

Henna has been used to beautify young women's bodies as part of social celebrations since the Bronze Age in the eastern Mediterranean. There are several texts, from Syria, talking about henna in the context of marriage and fertility celebrations. These texts, dating 1450-1200 BCE, are from the Ugaritic legend of Baal and Anath which is located in Mediterranean coast of Syria, a few kilometers north of the modern city of Latakia. These texts refer to women applying henna on their body, hands and feet in preparation to meet their husbands and Anath decorating herself with henna to celebrate a victory over the enemies of Baal. The legend of Baal is considered the oldest written reference to henna and its traditions.

It appears that there are earlier references to henna originating from Cyprus. Wall paintings found at Akrotiri, dated from 1680 BCE located in Cyprus show women with very similar markings like henna on their hands and feet. All these wall paintings describe weddings ceremonies or rituals. This early connection between young women and henna seems to be the origin of the Night of the Henna, which is now celebrated world-wide as the bride to be's "Hen night"

Night of Henna, also called Mehendi is celebrated traditionally the night before the wedding. The bride's family draws various designs on the bride body, hands and feet. This tradition is to symbolises the mysteries of married life. The Night of the Henna was celebrated by most groups in the areas where henna grew naturally. Regardless of the geographical location, Muslims, Hindus, Jews and Christians, all celebrated marriages by decorating the Bride and in some occasion the Groom, with henna.

The word Henna is from Arabic origin, from the word *Al-Hinna*. There are other names available such as Henne, Al-Khanna, Jamaica Mignonette, Egyptian Privet or Smooth Lawsonia. The real scientific name of Henna is *Lawsonia Enermis,* a plant which grows to be 4 to 8 feet high in hot climates and can be found in Iran, Pakistan, Syria, Morocco, Palestine, Yemen, Egypt, Uganda, Tanzania, Afghanistan, Senegal, Kenya, Ethiopia, Eritrea, and India.

Henna has been in the Middle East and Eastern Mediterranean history for more than 3500 years. Regardless of its true origin, henna seems to be very popular and continues to be very important in Arabian woman's way of life. Drawing henna on hands and feet might be different from region to region, but the colour and traditional methods of making the Henna remain the same.

23 ■ Why are Muslim women covered with Hijab ?

Hijab is the Arabic term for "cover". In some Arabic-speaking countries and Western countries, the word Hijab refers to women's head and face being covered. In Islam, Hijab has a much wider and deeper meaning. It means modesty, privacy, and morality. The word used in the Qur'an for a headscarf or veil is khimar. In some Arab countries, other words are used for head scarf such as Sheila.

The history of Hijab seems to be much older than Islam. This means women used to cover their faces long before Islam. In the Near East, Assyrian kings introduced both the privacy of women in the royal harem with the veil. Assyria was located between today's Iraq and Eastern Syria, 600BCE. This region is often referred to as the "Cradle of Civilization". Slaves had no right to cover their faces and were punished if they disobeyed this law.

Covering the face of woman seems to be a very old tradition not only related to Middle East. There are traces of Hijab in ancient Greece (776-323 BCE), in the Roman Christian world, in Persia and in India. All these civilizations had various form of Hijab covering upper class or royal women's faces and bodies.

Islam interpreted the tradition of the veil in its own way. Muslims in their first century (700 CE) at first were relaxed about women's dress codes. As Islam reached other lands, regional practices such as, the covering of women's face and body were gradually adopted. During the second Islamic century (800 CE), the veil became more common. From 10th to 15th century, the Islamic dress code was re-enforced for both men and women. Ibn Battuta (1304-1377 CE), a pioneer Arab traveler and explorer of the Islamic World, in the fourteenth century saw what he called a "remarkable thing"; "The Turkish women do not veil themselves. Not only royal ladies but also wives of merchants and common people will sit in a wagon drawn by horses. The windows are open and their faces are visible". His astonishment at the sight of these practices proves that Arabia was already using the veil extensively. It appears that between the 10th and 15th century, the Islamic principles were strictly applied and changed the dressing codes accordingly. Basically, Qu'ranic principles require men and women to dress modestly in public at all times.

As Hijab is the head covering, there are many traditional Islamic dressings to cover the rest of the body. Traditionally, Arabian women used to wear the "Sarwal", also called in some regions "Sharwal". Over the Sarwal, women wear the Jalebiya, a beautifully decorated long dress available in many colours and styles. On the top of Sarwal and Jalebiya, women wear what is known as Abaya. Abaya is usually a black, simple and loose long sleeves dress that covers the whole body including head, feet, and hands. Basically the Abaya is visible to everyone in public places, whereas the Jalebiya is visible to close family or her husband only. In the Muslim world, the Islamic dress is sometimes reinforced by the belief that the honor of the family depends on the woman remaining chaste. If the woman is violated in any way, the men of the family risk being seen as weak. For many women Islamic dressing reflects the belief that they are following God's commandments and dressing according to "the correct standard of modesty".

What constitutes modest clothing has changed over time. Like most customs, the dress reflects the practices of a region and the social position of the wearer. For example, in the United Arab Emirates, the Abaya is the national dress as a form of over-garment. The popular Abaya used to be made of thick materials such as jute. The high quality Abaya used to be made of Silk imported from India or Persia. Today, the Abaya is a fashion statement, a garment full of grace which cannot be ignored. There are some designer Abaya's, produced by international fashion industry leaders available at high price.

While Arabia has mastered the art of Hijab and veil in modern times, Europe is struggling to catch up and understand the Arabian life style. Hijab is considered as a very sensitive subject in the Western world. France in particular, has been the scene of many issues regarding the Hijab. In one hand, all French citizens are allowed to dress as they wish; part of personal freedom and human rights. In the other hand the Hijab is banned in schools and universities as it is the sign of religious belief. In France, all religious artifacts are banned within public areas regardless of the religion concerned.

Although laws of Hijab are strictly practiced, there is proof of active progress towards a modern Arabia through slight changes. Arabic women have created their own way of expression while respecting religious beliefs. Through understanding the meaning of Hijab culturally and socially, one cannot help but to respect the strong will of the Arab people to remain true to their beliefs and history.

24. ■Why do Arab men cover their head with a Khaffiyeh?

First of all, we need to distinguish between Khaffiyeh and Turban in terms of look, origin and usage.

A Khaffiyeh, also called Ghoudra, is a rectangular piece of cloth folded diagonally and draped over the men head. Yasser Arafat, the late Palestinian leader, made the Khaffiyeh famous in modern times. However, the Khaffiyeh is not solely Palestinian. Men in Jordan, Saudi Arabia and the Arab Gulf states wear Khaffiyehs in various colors and styles that are particular to their region.

I discovered four main types of Khaffiyeh: "Red and white", "black and white" and "white and white" all with patterns. Finally, there is also simple white colour Khaffiyeh without pattern. There are some other colours and patterns available but represent minorities. Jordanians, generally wear a red and white Khaffiyeh, while Palestinians wear black and white. Men from Saudi Arabia style the Khaffiyeh differently than a man from Jordan. The black cord that holds the Khaffiyeh is called an ekal. You might find other names for ekal in various regions. Some people say that the ekal used to be a camel retainer. Bedouins used to twist the ekal and put it around the Camels' front legs in order to stop the animal from walking far away at night. Regardless of the style, usage or colour, we can consider that today, the Khaffiyeh is worn by Muslims only.

Designed from a cloth of cotton, silk and sometimes synthetics, the turban is a long and narrow piece of cloth. It is crafted to wrap around the head, only held in place by its own tension. Although at times, a chin strap may be used to assist this.

The word turban in English comes from the Persian word, "dulband". What is very important for you to remember is that not everyone who wears a turban is a Muslim. In fact, Muslims don't all wear turbans. Indian Sikh's also wear the Turban, so it should not be considered an Islamic Symbol.

No one knows exactly when and where the turban and Khaffiyeh originated. Some 3,000 years old Assyrian carvings based in Iraq show Turbans on the heads of kings. Therefore, we can confirm existence of the Turban prior to Islam or Christianity. The Turban has evolved from a simple piece of clothing into something used to signify nobility and power.

Take for example a pair of shoes. While being a daily lifestyle item, over the years big name brands have been used to show your status in society. The more expensive the brand, the more money and power you must have. A similar thing has happened with Khaffiyehs and turbans. They have turned from being simple head coverings into an item that is a reflection of culture, political lines, and religion. While there is speculation that the Khaffiyeh finds its origins from the Turban there is no proof.

In practice, the Khaffiyeh is wrapped around the face and used as a protective gear in the desert to keep blowing sand out of the eyes. It also protects the head from the strong sunlight and other natural elements.

In Some occasion, the western media's tendency is to stereotype Khaffiyeh and Turban with terrorism. Images such as the Iran hostage crisis, with footage of Ayatollah Khomeini and his black turban have distressed the global media. Furthermore, images of Osama Bin Ladden on the most wanted FBI list covered with a Saudi Khaffiyeh has shocked and terrified the global population including Arabs.

Today, many Arab leaders use Khaffiyeh with very specific styling in order to represent their own country. In the United Arab Emirates and Saudi Arabia, wearing the Khaffiyeh is fully integrated within the cultural, traditional and religious layer of the society.

Younger generations of Arabs sometimes mix Arabic traditional dress and replace the Khaffiyeh with a modern baseball cap. A typical example is an Arabic dress, white dishdash (Long and straight man traditional dress), with a modern cap and sun glasses. In some occasions you might find young Arab men wearing the Khaffiyeh like a Turban. This is a very specific style and it appeared recently within the Arab fashion industry. I believe wearing the Khaffiyeh like a Turban is a statement, and proof that new generations are willing to evolve Arabic traditions with modern times. This evolution of style proves that Arabic societies are also fashion aware and open to changes.

25. ■ What is the difference between a Sheikh, Emir and Sultan?

Sheikh, Emir and Sultan are all from Middle Eastern origin and have been derived from the Arabic language. We will look into the details and the meaning of each of these words below. We can confirm that they are all three considered as "Titles" and define the status of the beholder. Additionally, there is no hierarchical relationship or ranking association between any of these three titles. The difference between Sheikh, Emir and Sultan is mostly related to the social affiliation of it's owner. I believe that we can simply associate the Sheikh to religious leaders whereas Emir is more appropriate to military leaders. Finally, Sultan is related to political leadership not only in the Arabic world but in other Islamic countries.

Sheikh is a word in the Arabic language meaning elder of a tribe, lord, admired wise man, or Islamic scholar. The daughter or wife of the Sheikh is called Sheikhah. Sheikh literally means "a man of old age", and it is used in that sense in Qur'anic Arabic. Later it came to be a title meaning leader, elder, or noble, especially in the Arabian Peninsula, where Sheikh became a traditional title of a Bedouin tribal leader in recent centuries. The most famous Sheikh of our time is probably late Sheikh Zayed bin Sultan al Nahyan, simply called Sheikh Zayed, the principal architect and ruler of United Arab Emirates.

Emir means in Arabic "commander" or "chieftain". Emir is derived from the Arabic root Amr, "command" and is considered as a military title. As matter of fact, Emir is a high title of nobility or office, used in Arabic nations of the Middle East and North Africa, and historically, in some Turkish states. The word Emir entered the English language in 1595 and is one of the titles or names of Prophet Mohammad during his life time. I found the word Emir pronounced Amir in some places of the Middle East. Amir and Amira mean Prince and Princess respectively.

The term Sultan is a title in Islam which in Arabic translates to "authority", "strength" or even "rulership". Originally, this word came from the Aramaic language, Sultana meaning "power". Sultan has several meanings in history, and soon become the title of various Muslim rulers. These rulers claimed sovereignty while renouncing the Caliphate. This term could also refer to a governor of a province located in the Caliphate.

I hope that you have a clear understanding of the difference between each of these titles. The clear segregation of these titles proves that Arabia is organized with defined hierarchy and classifications.

26. ■ Why do we weigh precious stones in Carat?

Today, the metric system is used by the majority of the people to measure weights, length, volume, distance, speed and many other elements of our daily life. Weights seem to have been standardized in Egypt long before length and other measures due to the importance of the commerce and good exchange. The oldest standard can be traced to 7000-8000 BCE. It was called the "bega" and was the smallest unit in a decimal system.

When Islam established itself on the Southern and Eastern Mediterranean coasts in the 7th century CE., it broke down many of the old commercial and political barriers between the Roman Empire and Arabia. As a result, a lot of new products came into the European market through Arabic-speaking trading businessmen. The words left their mark on European languages including English and French. Today, you can find many western words with Arabian origins.

The words "Carat" and "Karat" are both derived from "quirrat", which is Arabic for the seeds of the coral tree (Bean Seed). Although "Karat" and "Carat" have a common origin and are pronounced the same, they now have two different meanings.

Firstly, a "Carat" is the international unit of weight in gemstones. "Carat" was initially a unit of weight used by ancient merchants in the Middle East. It was the traditional weight measurement for precious stones such as diamonds and sapphires. Today, the carat is used as such for the weight of gem stones and was standardized internationally in 1913 at 0.2 grams. Most jewelery stores around the world sell diamonds and gems stones measured with Carats as the consumer feels purchasing a higher value of product. As an example, they will sell you a 5 Carats Diamond ring which represents only 1 gram. I can assure you that a 5 Carat Diamond is already a very large piece and very expensive.

Secondly, a Carat, originally spelt "Karat" is a unit for measuring the purity of gold and was established in 1555. The word Karat officially entered the English language in 1469. For gold, Karat has a totally different meaning than Carat for gemstones. The 'Karat' is one twenty-forth part a mix of gold and other metals. Therefore a 18 karat gold is 18 parts gold and 6 parts other metals, while pure gold is 24 karat. Many countries have their own ways of mixing the pure gold. As such, Swiss gold is mostly mixed with platinum for its strength and ability to be shaped and twisted. On the other hand, Indian gold is mostly pure and has a strong yellow colour.

Countries across the world allow different minimum karat standards. For example, in France and Italy the lowest permitted standard for gold is 18 karat, in Germany it is 8 karat and in the USA it is 10 karat gold. In UK, however, the minimum standard has been 9 karat since the First World War when gold was in short supply.

27 ■ Why are palm trees important in the Arabian lifestyle?

The earliest traces of palm trees are from Egypt and Persia 5000-6000 BCE in wild form. During the Bronze Age, around 4000 BCE, there are traces of palm tree farms in Southern Mesopotamia located in today's Iraq which is considered as Arabian territory. Obviously, these farms were producing dates. There are scripts available describing cultivation of Palm trees dated from 2500 BCE, found within the ancient Persian Empire, territories between today's Iraq and Iran. It seems that the Palm tree has a long history with the Middle Eastern civilization and traditions.

It is estimated that there are 90 million palm trees in the world and each tree can grow for more than 100 years. 64 million of these trees are grown in Arab countries, which produce 2 million tons of dates every year. The palm tree requires high temperatures and low air humidity to produce dates.

The date palm is very important to the people of the desert and arid lands such as North Africa and the Middle East. As a result, every part of the palm tree has its uses and makes the palm tree an important part of the Arabian daily life. The wood and leaves provide timber and fabric for houses and fences. The leaves are used for making ropes, cords, baskets and furniture. Bases of the leaves and the fruit are used as fuel. The palm fruit provides food products such as date vinegar, date chutney, paste for bakery products and additional flavoring for oranges, bananas and almonds. Some of the most traditional Bedouin dishes are based on the date. The Arabian-flavored Bedouin dish known as Canua and roasted whole date seeds is the perfect example of the importance of Palm tree in the Arabian traditions.

The Palm tree and dates are carefully considered in Qur'an. It is mentioned that palm tree is clearly a positive and important piece of the Arabian living: "*Shake the trunk of the palm tree towards thee: it will drop fresh, ripe dates upon thee. Eat, then, and drink, and let thine eye be gladdened!*" (Qur'an 19:25-26) Prophet Mohammad also said: "*There is among trees one that is pre-eminently blessed, as is the Muslim among men; it is the date palm*".

Iraq is the top commercial producer and exporter of dates, closely followed by Saudi Arabia, Egypt and Algeria. In Saudi Arabia, Madinah's date market is called "Souq Al Tumoor" where you can find more than 150 varieties of dates. Apparently the most popular and expensive date is called Anbara. There are a total of more than 600 type of dates produced across the Middle East. Palm trees start producing after 4-5 years and reach full production after 10-12 years.

It appears that the date has a lot of benefits for the human body, a proven fact, agreed upon by many nutritionists. The sugar content of the date is about 80%; the rest consists of protein, fat and minerals including copper, sulfur, iron, magnesium and fluoric acid. Dates are high in fiber and an excellent source of potassium. Five dates (approx. 45 grams) contain about 115 calories, nearly all from carbohydrates. Bedouin Arabs, who eat them on a regular basis, show an extremely low incidence rate of cancer and heart diseases. Iraqi's have mastered the Art of date, going beyond date-dishes and date-pastries. Some Iraqi's distil their own Arak Liquor from dates.

A study conveyed by Dubai Chamber of Commerce and Industry disclosed that there are around 40 million palm trees in the UAE, and that 40% percent of this number is in Al Ain. Some of these trees are part of plantations, a decisive step made in the UAE to combat climate change and desertification and to ensure the well being of UAE's environment. Much of this tree-planting is due to the support of Sheikh Zayed bin Sultan Al Nahyan, late President of the UAE, a true environmentalists and visionary personality. Considering the fact that the population of the UAE is around 4 million, there are 10 palm trees per person.

28. ■ What is the origin of Shisha?

Depending on your geographical location, shishas are known as other names, such as a nargeeleh, arghileh, Hookah, okka, water pipe, kalyan, ghelyoon, ghalyan or hubbly bubbly.

The archaic form of this name, *hookah* is most commonly used in English for historical reasons. The word *Shisha* is derived from an Arabic term for a water pipe. The substance smoked with the Shisha is usually called tobamel or maassel. The Shisha can be used for smoking many substances, such as herbal fruits, tobacco, or cannabis.

In the Middle East, shredded tobacco has long been mixed with sweeteners such as honey, molasses, sugar or semi-dried fruit. Many contemporary manufacturers use glycerin as the primary sweetener in shisha due to its low cost and humectant qualities. The practice of adding strong flavors is a relatively recent one but has grown in popularity in the past 20 years.

There are various hypotheses regarding the birthplace of Shisha. I found roots in America, India and Persia (Iran). The American and Indian tracks lack sources. Two thousand years before the discovery of shisha, it seems that a water pipe called Dhoom Netra, filled with aromatic and medicinal herbs, and also very probably with drugs, was smoked in America by the Indian Americans. Very similar practices using coconut shells as the container for smoking medical herbs has been discovered in India.

Although we are unsure of the true origin of the water pipe, it is believed that the original design for the Shisha came from Persia and completed its revolution in Turkey.

Turks reshaped the design and added a hose around 500 years ago. To this day, the same basic design is used for each Shisha. During the 17th century, Shisha pipes were often seen in coffee shops or small restaurants along the streets of Turkey and other Middle Eastern countries. Since then the world of Shisha smoking has greatly expanded.

Shisha and the act of smoking one has become a favorite Middle Eastern pastime and it's practice is spreading throughout the world. This, for some, is more appealing than cigarette or cigar smoking because it contains only 0.5% nicotine and no tar. With a vast collection of flavors to choose from and many other variables to manipulate, hookah smoking is truly an art.

Shisha is from the Persian word shishe (literally translated as glass and not bottle). Hashish is an Arabic word for grass, which may have been another way of saying tobacco. Another source states, "In early Arabic texts, the term hashish referred not only to cannabis resin but also to the dried leaves or flower heads and sweetmeats made with them". The word Hookah itself may stem from Arabic uqqa, meaning small box, pot, or jar. Both names refer to the original methods of constructing the smoke and water chambers of the hookah.

There is no discrimination when it comes to smoking the hookah, as men and women equally partake in this important social activity.

Today, you can find hookahs in homes and restaurants around the world. Shisha is a mixture of tobacco and treacle, honey or sugar, and distilled water with fruit flavors. Shisha tobacco is very light and flavorful with a wonderful fruity aroma.

29 ■ Who is Prophet Mohammad?

According to Muslims, Mohammad is the "Last" Prophet. He was born in Mecca in 570 CE and was a member of the Quraysh tribe which was in control of the city of Mecca located in today's Saudi Arabia. We will look into this question in a factual way in order to respect all opinions.

The name Mohammad means "the praised one" in Arabic. Within Islam, Mohammad is known as Nabi which means Prophet and Rasul which means the Messenger. In the Qur'an, in verse 33:40, it singles out Mohammad as the "Seal of the Prophets". The Qur'an refers to Mohammad as "Ahmad" (61:6) Arabic for "more praiseworthy".

As with Moses and Jesus, we know little about his childhood. Mohammad was son of Abdullah and Aminah. His father died shortly before his birth, and he lost his mother at the age of six. As a young orphan, he was raised by his uncle, for whom he worked as a shepherd. At age 9, Mohammad joined his uncle on a caravan travelling to Syria.

As a young man, Mohammad worked as a camel driver between Syria and Arabia. He established a career managing caravans on behalf of merchants. Mohammad met many people from different nationalities and faiths. He was exposed to Jews, Christians and pagans.

At age 25, Mohammad was employed by Khadija, a wealthy Meccan widow who was involved in trade and business. Despite the 15 years age difference, the two were married and enjoyed a loving and happy marriage.

It is believed that Mohammad miraculously started receiving the divine words of God transmitted by Archangel Gabriel over the last 23 years of his life. It is believed that Gabriel, called Jibril in Arabic, is the highest ranked Archangel and he is the Angel that serves as a messenger of God. The content of these revelations, known as the Qur'an, was memorized and recorded by his followers and compiled into a single holy book shortly after his death. The language of Qur'an is Arabic and is considered as the most complete and advanced Arabic text ever written. Taking into consideration that Mohammad could not read or write, this was a miracle. The foundation of the Islamic Theology is based on the Qur'an and details of Mohammad's life as recounted by his biographers and his contemporaries. The word Qur'an is derived from Arabic word *qaraa* which means "to read, or recitation". All followers of Islam are called Muslims.

Muslims do not regard Mohammad as the founder of a new religion but as the restorer of the original monotheistic faith of Adam, Abraham and other Prophets, whose messages, according to some, had become misinterpreted or corrupted over time. Monotheism is from Greek word meaning One God.

Allah is the Arabic term for God. The word was used for local Gods in Arabia before Mohammad began to use it for the one God who revealed His messages to him. All Muslims believe in One God, in Angels, in the revealed books, in the Prophets and in Judgment Day.

In 622 CE, Mohammad left Mecca for an Oasis called Yathrib. The name of this oasis was later changed to Madinah al-Nabi to commemorate Mohammad's association with the city. The Arabic name given to Madinah means the "City of the Messenger of God".

In the year 630 CE, Mohammad and his military forces marched to Mecca and defeated it, and rededicated the Kaba temple to Allah. Mohammad witnessed the conversion to Islam of nearly the entire Meccan population, and then returned to Madinah. Mohammad died in 632 CE having conquered nearly all of Arabia for Islam.

Within 100 years of Mohammad's death, Islam reached the Atlantic in one direction and borders of China in the other. This success was due in large part to the military and political abilities of Mohammad's successors, the Caliphs.

30. ■ What is the difference between a Sunni and

Shia Muslim?

In order to provide you a clear understanding; we will stick to facts. Both Sunni and Shia Muslims share the Quaranic fundamental Islamic beliefs and articles of faith. In other words, Sunni and Shia followers are all bound to Qur'an. Sunni Muslims make up the majority of Muslims all over the world. More than 900 Million Muslims are Sunni and 120 Millions are Shia. Most populations of Shia Muslims can be found in Iran, Iraq, Lebanon and Yemen.

The difference between Sunni's and Shia's originally started not from spiritual differences, but political ones. Sunni and Shia's division goes back to the death of Mohammad. People began to question who should be the chosen one to lead the people in the newly formed religion of Islam.

Those Sunni Muslims believed the best practice was to find those who were capable of doing the job and elect one of them. It was a result of this that Prophet Mohammad's adviser and friend, Abu Bakr became the very first Caliph of the Islamic nation.

The word "Sunni" in Arabic comes from a word meaning "one who follows the traditions of the Prophet", it can be directly translated to "tradition".

On the other hand, Shia Muslims believe that leadership should have stayed within the Prophet's own family, among those specifically appointed by him, or among Imams appointed by God Himself. The Shia Muslims believe that following the Prophet Mohammad's death, leadership should have passed directly to his cousin and son-in-law, Ali. Throughout history, Shia Muslims have not recognized the authority of elected Muslim leaders, choosing instead to follow a line of Imams which they believe have been appointed by the Prophet Mohammad or God Himself. The word "Shia" in Arabic means "party of people", it can be translated to "partisans". These are the followers of "Ahl-al-Bayt". In fact, the term "Shia" is a shortened version of the word "Shia-t-Ali" which is translated into "the Party of Ali".

Shia Muslims reject traditions such as Hadith, the Ancient Muslim Scripts, and do not base any of their religious practices on the testimony of Sunni leaders. As a result, there are some differences in religious practice between Shia and Sunni Muslims such as prayer, fasting, pilgrimage, etc. We can compare the difference between Shia and Sunni the same way that Christian Catholic is different to Protestants.

Sunni's and Shia's share common major holidays such as Eid al-Adha, the festival of Sacrifice and Eid al-Fitr, the Festival of the Breaking of the Fast followed after the Ramadan period.

It is important to remember that despite all of these differences in opinion and practice, Shia and Sunni Muslims share the main articles of Islamic belief. In fact, most Muslims call themselves simply, "Muslims". Regardless of their origin, location, language, political alliances, they all believe in the holy Qur'an, the foundation of Islam.

31. ■ Where does the name Dubai come from?

You might see the word Dubai spelled Dubayy in various scripts or official documents. There are two Dubai cities, one in the United Arab Emirates and one in the Al Dahna' region of Saudi Arabia, between Riyadh and Ad Dammam. Obviously, we refer to Dubai in United Arab Emirates which is considered as the greatest place in the Middle East. Dubai is located on the northeast coast of the United Arab Emirates and is roughly at 16 meter above sea level. Dubai shares borders with Abu Dhabi in the south, Sharjah in northeast and the Sultanate of Oman in the southeast. The emirate of Dubai covers only an area of 4,114 km^2 (1,588 mi^2).

There are several theories as to how Dubai was named. You can decide and draw your own conclusions.

The first theory is that the word Dubai is from Persian origin, a combination of the Farsi words related to two brothers referring to Deira and Bur Dubai.

The second theory is based on words. Dubai was under the protection of the United Kingdom by the "Exclusive Agreement" of 1892, agreeing to protect Dubai against any attacks from the Ottoman Empire. British military used to ask the Bedouins directions such as "The Bay?" Therefore, some people believe the word dubai come from "The bay" as it was the main port for merchandise and goods. At this time, Dubai was referred to as "Al Wasl" in books by British historians and geographical records including the present-day areas of Jumeirah, Shindagha, Deira and Bur Dubai. There are other theories available and all proposed hypothesis have probably some historical truth.

Historical facts, scripts, maps and books are the most reliable source of information. We are unable to confirm the origin of the name "Dubai" but we can confirm the following;

The earliest records that mention Dubai is from 1095 CE, in the "Book of Geography" ("Mojam Ma Ostojam men Asmae Al belaad wal Mawadhea") by the Spanish-Arab geographer and historian, Abu Abdullah al-Bakri. (1014–1094 CE). He refers to Dubai as a vast place. Al-Bakri spent his entire life in Spain and never traveled to the locations of which he wrote.

The Venetian pearl merchant Gaspero Balbi visited the Dubai region in 1580 CE and mentioned Dubai (*Dibei*) for its pearling industry described Venetian pearl divers. As a matter of fact, Dubai has been for centuries the hub for pearl and gold exchange between East and West.

Today, Dubai is a man made wonderland where the authorities have extraordinary vision. As the Emirate of Dubai has an insufficient reservoir of Petrol to generate future revenue for the federal government, the ruling authorities have decided to change the income revenue focus of Dubai from Petrol to many other revenue streams such as real estate, tourism, finance, infrastructure, telecommunication and more. Today, Dubai has the tag of "Business Tourism", a relatively new concept where business is done in a very relaxed and luxurious environment.

Personally, I don't believe any of these explanations are completely accurate, but perhaps only fragments of the truth of it's origin. In my opinion, as per the historical scripts available, the name of Dubai has existed for more than 1000 years.

32. ■ Why is the Islamic Calendar different than the Christian Calendar?

The Muslim era is dated from the Hegira calendar, also called the Hijri calendar. The main difference between Islamic and Christian calendars is the fact that it depends on the moon where as Christian calendar depends on the sun. This lunar calendar has 12 months that are calculated based on the motion of the moon. The Hijri calendar is approximately 11 days shorter than the Christian calendar (365 days) which is based on the rotation of the sun. The twelve Hijri months are equivalent to 12 x 29.53 = 354.36 days. The Islamic calendar is based on the Qur'an (Soura 9, 36-37) and it applies to all Muslims and religious events.

In the year 639 CE, Caliph Umar I created the original Hijri calendar. He started the Hijri calendar on 16 July 622, A.H 1 (Anno Hegirae) which is the first year of the Muslim calendar, the year when Prophet Mohammad moved from Mecca to Madinah. The years were then numbered with acronym "A.H" for the Latin word Anno Hegirae, the year of the Hijra.

I have used the annotation CE and BCE for all historical references. CE means "Common Era", which replaces AD (Anno Domini, "The Year of the Lord"). BCE stands for "Before Common Era", which replaces BC (Before

105

Christ) in most books. I believe CE and BCE should be used for all international books instead of AD or AH to simplify all chronological and historical events and avoid religious interference with historical facts.

The Islamic calendar is the official calendar in countries around the Gulf, especially Saudi Arabia. Some Muslim countries use the Christian (Gregorian) calendar for civil purposes and only turn to the Islamic calendar for religious purposes. The names of the 12 months of the Islamic year are: (Other spellings are possible)

1	Muharram	7	Rajab
2	Safar	8	Sha'ban
3	Rabi' al-awwal (Rabi' I)	9	Ramadan
4	Rabi' al-thani (Rabi' II)	10	Shawwal
5	Jumada al-awwal (Jumada I)	11	Dhu al-Qi'dah
6	Jumada al-thani (Jumada II)	12	Dhu al-Hijjah

In the year 2010 we started the Islamic year 1431. Note that although since 622 and 2010, 1388 years have passed in the Christian calendar; 1431 years have passed in the Islamic calendar. This is because its year is shorter by about 11 days than the Christian calendar year. Therefore, the Islamic years are slowly gaining in on the Christian years. Yet, it will be many years before the two match. The 1st day of the 5th month of CE 20874 in the Christian calendar will also be the 1st day of the 5th month of AH 20874 of the Islamic calendar.

Saudi Arabia bases their calendar on a calculated astronomical moon. Since 1999 (AH 1420) Saudi Arabia started using the following rule: On the 29th day of any Islamic month, the times when the sun and the moon set are compared. If the sun sets before the moon, the next day will be the first of a new month; but if the moon sets before the sun, the next day will be the last day (30th) of the current month. This can somehow become an issue when trying to predict national public holidays. If you work in the Middle East, you will notice that the holidays are only announced a few days prior to the date as the scholars are not sure which day the holiday will occur.

There are some simplified techniques to predict the dates. All odd numbered months have 30 days and all even numbered months have 29 days with an extra day added to the last month in 'leap years'. Using the above rules, such calendar would give an average month length of 29.53056 days, which is quite close to the lunar month of 29.53059 days, so *on the average*, it would be a quite accurate estimation.

Finally, I personally believe that Calendars are just a measurement tool for time. There are many calendars available with various start dates, cycles and rules. The Hijri Calendar fits the purpose of the Islamic world. Did you notice that December is the 12th month of the year? December comes from the Latin word "Dec" which means ten. Why then is the number 10 represented as the 12th month of Christian Calendar?

33 ■ Do Muslims believe in Angels?

We can confirm that Jews, Christians and Muslims, all believe in Angels and in some extent the different hierarchy and ranking that is applied to them. As per Torah, the book of Jews, Hebrews believe that there are four Archangels, Michael, Gabriel, Raphael, and Uriel. Christians believe in only two, Michael and Gabriel.

It is also proven that Muslims do believe in Angels, and call them by their Arabic name "Mala'ikah". The word is sometimes interpreted as meaning "messenger". It's historical roots come from the word "alk" which is simply "to send".

There is however, some belief the word actually comes from the term "he controlled" or "malaka" in Arabic. This is because the belief is that many of these Angels have a power that control over the physical world.

Both possible meanings are still consistent with the Muslim concept of Angels as spiritual beings sent by God to bring the message of Allah to earth.

In Islam and as per Qur'an a Hafaza is a type of Angel. We can consider a Hafaza equivalent to the Christian concept of a guardian Angel. Each person is assigned with four Hafazas, two of which keep watch during the day and two during the night. They help the soul fight attacks from Shaitan, the Devil. The Hafazas keep track of each and every good and bad actions and record them all in their books. On Qiyamah, Judgement day, they will be used to judge if the person is worthy of admission into the Paradise.

Angels in Islam are believed to be light-based creatures, created from light, by God to serve and worship Him. Belief in Angels is one of the six Articles of Faith in Islam, without which there is no faith. The six Articles are belief in: God, His Angels, His Books, His Messengers, the Last Day, and that predestination, both good and evil, comes from God.

There is no standard hierarchical organization in Islam that distinguishes Angels and Archangels. Most Islamic scholars agree that this is an unimportant topic in Islam, especially since such a topic has never been directly mentioned or addressed in the Qur'an.

However, it is clear that there is a set order and hierarchy that exists between Angels. It is agreed that Archangels are the highest order of Angels. The word Archangel derives from the Greek Archangelos. Arch means "primary" or "chief" and Angelos means "messenger". There are four Archangels acknowledge by Muslims:

- **Jibra'il** also known as Gabriel in English. Jibra'il is the Archangel responsible for revealing the Qur'an to Mohammad, verse by verse. Jibra'il is known as the Angel who acts as intermediary between God and man. He is mentioned many times specifically in the Qur'an.

- **Azrael** is not mentioned in Qur'an or Hadith. Long before the creation of man, Azrael was the only Angel who ventured down to the Earth. It was there it faced the wicked Iblis, or the devil. The journey was done to bring God the materials he needed to begin creating man. Because of this the Angel, known then as Azreal became the Angel of death.

- **Mika'il** (or Michael or Michel). Mika'il is the Archangel charged with bringing thunder and lightning onto the Earth. The single allusion to Mika'il in the Qur'an (2:98) states: *"Whoever is an enemy to Allah or his Angels or his apostles or Jibra'il or Mika'il, verily Allah is an enemy of the unbelievers."*

- **Israfil,** also known as Raphael. According to the Hadith, Israfil is the Angel responsible for signaling the coming of Judgment Day by blowing a horn from a holy rock in Jerusalem and sending out a Blast of Truth. This has been described in many places in Qur'an

Finally, Angels within Islam are intangible and created for the sole purpose of serving Allah. Being made of light, they can assume almost any form, completely real to the human eye, and traverse a distance just as fast as light or faster. The interesting part is that Christians, Jews and Muslims believe all in the same Angels and agree that Gabriel is the most important of all.

34. ■ Why do Muslims pray so much?

Some westerners might feel that Muslims pray a lot, probably more than other religions. This is because we see Muslims pray several times a day. Islamic prayers are based on strict rules and are designed to provide a discipline to the Muslim daily life. These short prayers provide small breaks, allowing all Muslims to invest into their personal beliefs everyday of the week. In many Muslim countries, during informal business meetings, you might notice that the host leaves the gathering to join the prayer for few minutes. At first, this might feel shocking to newcomer foreigners but it is common practice in many Arabic countries. I have personally seen in many occasions that meetings are avoided or delayed around 1:30 pm as it corresponds to the midday prayer time.

So, how many times must Muslims pray per day? Muslims are demanded by the Qur'an to perform "Salat" five times a day. Five distinctive prayers from early morning till night form the daily Muslim investment into their beliefs. The word "Salat" means prayer in Classical and Qur'anic Arabic. There are strict rules and regulations that apply to the daily prayers. First of all, the prayers are obligatory to every Muslim above the age of puberty, with the exception of mentally or physically ill persons. Secondly there are specific timings for each prayer, which integrate the Islamic beliefs deep into their daily lives. Each of these five prayers corresponds to a specific time called "waqt" in which they must be performed, unless there is a very good reason for not being able to perform them on time. There are 5 Waqt per day, called Fajr

(Dawn prayer), Dhuhr (Mid-day prayer), Asr (Afternoon prayer), Maghrib (Sunset prayer), and Isha'a (Night prayer).

Salat may be classified into four categories of obligation: fard, wajib, sunnah and nafil. There are additional prayers that at times are offered. These known voluntary prayers must be done after the required prayers have been completed. Sunni Muslims refer to these as "sinnah" while the Shi'a Muslims know them as "nafil".

All Muslims ask for Allah to show them the "right path" as mentioned in Soura al-Fatihah which is recited in every prayer. In addition, in the Qur'an it is mentioned that: (8:2) "The true believers are those who feel a fear in their hearts (of the consequences of violating the commands of God) when God is mentioned. And when His Revelations are recited to them, they find their faith strengthened. They do their best and then put their trust in their Lord."

Raka'ah are the units of prayer in the Salat. Each of the raka'ah does contain different positions that transition from one post to another to match different verses of the holy book the Qur'an. The raka'ah begins with the worshiper standing and ends as they are in a prostrate position. Depending on which type prayer the participant is doing, there are numerous times each raka'ah might be done.

Most importantly the practice of Salat is performed as one faces the direction of Qibla. This is in the general direction of the Ka' ba in Mecca.

Commonly throughout Arabia, you can find the direction of Qibla in all hotels and resting places indicated by a discreet pointer. In many airplanes (Middle Eastern Airlines), electronic compasses with individual screens display Qibla's direction at all times so Muslims can pray regardless of the airplane's direction.

Interestingly, it appears that Muslims suffer less from backache and joint related diseases as they have physical exercise during the prayer, bending their body and resting their forehead on the floor several times as sign of respect to God. Such movements, exercised several times a day, become a real advantage to Muslims health.

During this time, the prayers of the Muslim provide a reminder to be thankful for their blessings. It also ensures that Islam becomes the priority of the Muslim over everything else. While doing this they agree to submit to God's will and dedicate their life to him.

In conclusion, I believe the daily Islamic prayers start and end each Muslims daily life. This is the proof that contrary to Christianity; the Islamic belief is firmly lived all day long by all Muslims. It provides Muslim a healthy lifestyle starting the day early and finishing also early.

35. ■ What is Ramadan?

Eid al-Fitr stands for "Festival of the Breaking of the Fast" in the Arabic language and is one of Islam's two major festivals. It marks the end of Ramadan, the holy month of fasting, and is celebrated during the first three days of the month of Shawwal.

A communal prayer at daybreak on the first day kicks off this festival. This time is spent with friends, and gifts are exchanged while new clothes are worn. Also time is made to visit the graves of deceased relatives. During this time the traditional greeting for the 'Eid Al-Fitr is "Eid Mabarak" which means "May God make it a blessed feast".

During the Hijri Calendar, the ninth month is called Ramadan. The roots of this word is from the Arabic term "Ramad" which translated to mean "dryness".

Ramadan is the holy month of fasting for adult Muslims and was established by the Prophet Mohammad in the year 638 CE. As the Hijri Calendar has 354 days, Ramadan occurs about 11 days earlier each year and is never the same day of the year. It has a cycle of 33 years before happening on the same day again.

Ramadan is the fourth pillar of Islam and most importantly it is the month when Qur'an was revealed to Prophet Mohammad. Therefore, it is considered the most blessed and sacred month during an Islamic's year. During this time, fasting, self-accountability, prayers, charity and other forms of religious observation are recommended at this time. Ramadan is set to remain a scared time and followers are to obey God's prescription for adhering to the daily fasting. Especially stressed at this time; religious observances associated with Ramadan are kept throughout the month. Muslims are to follow this from the time the moon appears to be full.

During this time, from dawn until sunset sexual activities, drinking, smoking and eating are all prohibited. It is during Ramadan that the Muslim is to focus their time on the Islamic faith and teachings. This means they should not engage in greed, lust, gossip and other forms of prohibited actions. It is also encouraged that the devoted read the Qur'an and increase their faith values.

The month of Ramadan is a great time to visit Muslim countries. The working hours are changed and usually most people work a few hours less during this period. Additionally, shops and shopping malls are open very late night to accommodate the Ramadan specific working hours. I noticed that the Muslim daily habits are changed during the Holy month. I would suggest you react softly to any business during the Ramadan period. Most jobs are late or pending, phone calls are not answered on time and business feels slower than ever. The working hours are unclear and depend on each individual business. I suggest you simply take advantage of the Holy Ramadan as a time to simply look into and gain respect and understanding for the Islamic religion and traditions.

With the Islamic holiday called Eid al-Fitr, it marks the end of the prescribed fasting period and on the first day of the next month called Shawwal, after another new moon has been sighted. Eid al-Fitr means the "Festival of Breaking the Fast". In many countries, Arabs call it simply Eid. The first Eid was celebrated in 624 CE by Mohammad with his companions and relatives after winning the Battle of Badr. Food is donated to the poor ('Zakat al-Fitr') and everyone puts on their best clothing to attend communal prayers held in the early morning. This is followed by feasting and visiting relatives and friends.

36. ■ Where is Mecca and why is it the symbol of Islam?

Mecca is located in Saudi Arabia, about 80Km from the Red Sea Coast, around a natural well, with 1.6 million inhabitants. Mecca is the most holy city in Islam. The city is revered as being the first place created on earth, as well as the place where Prophet Ibrahim together with his son Isma'il, built the Ka'ba. The Ka'ba is the central worship site of Islam, a rectangular building made of bricks.

Around the Ka'ba is the great mosque, al-Haram, and around the mosque, in between the mountains, are the houses that make up the city of Mecca.

Mecca was a central point on the caravan routes running over the Arabian Peninsula at the time of Prophet Mohammad and was considered as a holy city even before the first revelations. It was during this time that a revelation was given to the Prophet Mohammad in Ghare Hera. Hera is located in Jabl-e-Noor on the roadway to Mina about 5 km to the East of Holy city of Mecca.

Mecca, while an important place should not be exaggerated as the absolute centre of the Muslim religion. The main religious centres moved from Mecca easily on. Mecca retains its importance by being the destination for pilgrimage, and the focal point for the dedicated Muslims.

Today, many of the people living in Mecca are pilgrims wanting to study Islam in the very centre of the world. This learning is primarily aimed at average people, and even today deeper Muslim theology is explored in other places outside of Mecca.

Apart from the services for pilgrimage there are only modest economic activities to maintain daily routines. Every year more than 2 million pilgrims attend the Hajj. The number of pilgrims is currently regulated; each country can only send a fixed number of pilgrims every year.

Mecca used to be called Macoraba. Once under the control of Mohammad (630), Mecca was purged from all non-Muslim religion. Between 1269 to 1517, political Mecca shifted from Egyptian Mamluks control to Ottoman Empire. Finally, King Ibn Saud, the father of Saudi Arabia takes control over Mecca in 1925. Since then few minor architectural enhancements have been applied to Mecca, leaving it primarily unchanged over the last century.

37 ■ Who created Saudi Arabia?

During pre-modern times, local and foreign rulers fought for control of the Arabian Peninsula region. In 1517 the Ottoman Empire gained control of most of the region, which affected the geographical and political scene.

Saudi Arabia is a new nation in the scheme of things. With origins dating back to the puritanical Wahhabit movement in the 18th century, it was then it gained allegiance with the Saud family. Much of the support came from a Bedouin following; the Sauds obtained control of the peninsula, with the exception of Yemen and Hadhramaut.

However, in 1811 The Wahhabi movement was stopped by the Egyptian expedition led by the songs of Mohammad Ali. They were revived in the middle 1800's only to again be defeated in 1891 by the Rashid.

Abd al-Aziz ibn Saud (1880-1953), better known as Ibn Saud, is a descendant of the first Wahhabi rulers. He is responsible for developing the current Saudi Arabia. Known as the first king, and often considered the father of Saudi Arabi. By 1902 Ibn Saud conquered Riyadh was ruler of the Nejd by 1906. Known as a great strategist, he often proved his skills with great thinking and knowledge which can't be said about many 22 year olds!

Just before World War I, Ibn Saud dominated the region of Al-Hasa. During this time, he extended his military control over the neighboring areas, and proceeded in his conquest of the Hejaz. As 1925 approached, the city of Mecca was in turn conquered. Shortly following this, the two kingdoms became the Kingdom of Saudi Arabia. This in 1932 under Islamic Law, created absolute monarchy, and the first King of this newly formed kingdom was Ibn Saud.

As of recently, the green and white flag used by Saudi Arabia was introduced on March 15, 1973. On it is an Arabic Inscription along with a beautiful sword. The script on the flag is written in the Thuluth script (a variety of Arabic calligraphy, which made its first appearance in the fourth century known as one of the hardest Arabic scripts to write). It is the shahada or Islamic declaration of faith: "There is no God but God; Mohammad is the Messenger of God". A green flag with the shahada is in relation with the 18th Century Wahhabi movement and associated with the Saud family's rise to power in 1902.

38. ■ What is a Masjid?

The Arabic word masjid is originated from the Arabic verb sajada which means "to bow" or "to kneel" in reference to the ritual performed during Islamic prayers.

The term used for the place where Islamic believers come together for their prayer is called the mosque. Muslims often refer to the mosque by its Arabic name, "masjid". The word masjid has origins from Aramaic. It is proven to be linked to "m-s-g-d" which roots back to the 5th century BCE. It means in general terms "place of worship", but has also been shown to mean "sacred pillar".

The word used in the Qur'an to call the sanctuary of Kaaba in the city of Mecca is "masjid". In comparison, the Qur'an uses the word "masjid" to describe the places of worship for various religions.

The term "Mosque" is a reference to the various types of buildings for Islamic worship. Another of the distinctions that can be used is between a larger mosque called "masjid jami" which has a larger sized community and more amenities.

According to Islam, the first house of God in the world was the Kaaba, which was built by Abraham upon an order from God. Known as the oldest Islamic-built mosque's the Quba Mosque is located in Madinah. However, during his time in Mecca, Mohammad determined the Kaaba to be the primary mosque and it is considered to be the single holiest place.

The qibla, the direction Muslims face during prayer, is the direction from their location on Earth towards the Kaaba. It is around the Kaaba that ritual circumambulation (the act of moving around a sacred object) is performed by Muslims during the Hajj (pilgrimage) season as well as during the Umrah (lesser pilgrimage).

In 630 CE, as Mohammad conquered the city of Mecca, he in turn converted Kaaba to a mosque. In recent times this has become known as the sacred mosque. During this time, it has been expanded on, and has seen improvements to accommodate the growing number of Muslims who lived in the area, or made their regular pilgrimages. Today, the Sacred Mosque in Mecca, the Masjid al-Nabawi in Madinah and Al Aqsa in Jerusalem are considered the three holiest sites in Islam.

39 ■ Where is Al Madinah?

Madinah, also known as Al Madinah is a City in Saudi Arabia with an estimated 890,000 inhabitants (2003 estimate). Situated in Hijaz, in western Saudi Arabia, 160 km from the Red Sea coast, at an elevation of 625 meters. Madinah has excellent road connections with other urban centres of Saudi Arabia. The word Madinah in Arabic simply means, "City".

Madinah is ranked as the 2nd most holy place in Islam, due to being the place where Islam first established itself, and where Prophet Mohammad died and was buried. 18th Soura's of Qur'an were revealed in Madinah and they are called by Muslims Madinah Souras. Formerly it was referred to as either Al Madinah Al-Munawwara, 'The Luminous City', or Madinah Rasul Allah, 'City of God's Prophet'. Al Madinah is short for 'Madinat an-Nabiy', 'Prophet's Town'.

Only Muslims are allowed to enter Madinah. While people can see this city from their airplanes through the airport, it is only because it is just outside the sacred city limits.

Madinah has a very long history. Late 1st millennium BCE Yathrib Jews settled in the Madinah oasis. At this time,

Madinah was called Yathrib. It was around 400 CE, that king of Sabaean converts the city of Yathrib and converts the city to the Judaism. It is then designated as the State's religion.

In 622 CE, the Hijra, the Muslim community settled in Yathrib and represented only a minority of the population. Their numbers would rapidly increase over the years.

In 627 CE, all members of the Jewish tribe (Banu Qurayza) are executed by the Muslims, following their support for the Meccans during the Battle of the Trench. Finally, around 630 CE, 'Madinat an-Nabiy' becomes effective name of Yathrib. Since this time, Madinah is an Islamic town and the focal-point of Muslim religion.

Finally, the Madinah was conquered by the Wahhabis in 1804. In 1925 Madinah surrenders to the control of King Ibn Saud, the father of the current Kingdom of Saudi Arabia. Since then Madinah has kept all it splendor and magnificence.

Considered the most important of all historical and religious buildings, the Prophet's Mosque is the location where Prophet Mohammad is buried. There is however some interest in The Mosque of the Two Qiblahs as it commemorates the change in prayers from Jerusalem to the current Mecca. One final point of interest to be mentioned is the burial place of Mohammad's uncle that died during the Battle of Uhud. His tomb is called the Tomb of Hamza.

Today, Madinah city attracts many pilgrims. They visit Madinah after performing the Hajj or Umra in Mecca.

40. ■Where is the smallest mainland Arabic country?

The Arab world consists of twenty-two countries stretching from Mauritania in the West to Oman in the East. They have a combined population of 323 million people.

Today, the smallest autonomous mainland Arab country in the Middle East is Lebanon with only 10,452 square kilometers and a population of an estimated 4 Million.

The most ancient scripts carrying the word LBN on three of these twelve tablets that make up the Epic of Gilgamesh, an epic poem from Babylon dated 2900 BCE. LBN is also mentioned in the texts of the library of Ebla, an ancient city located in northern Syria, about 55 km southwest of Aleppo (2400 BCE). Additionally, the word Lebanon is also mentioned in the Bible, in fact there are 71 different times it is mentioned in the text of the Old Testament.

Lebanon was the original homeland of the ancient Phoenicians. Phoenicians lived around the Eastern Mediteranean sea long before the rise in power of Cyrus the Great, who was the founder of Persian Empire also called

Kurosh-e Bozorg (576-530 BCE). After these two centuries being under Persian rule, Alexander the Great (Megas Alexandros; 356, 323 BCE) went into battle and burned Tyre, which was the capital Phoenician city. During the following centuries leading up to recent times, Lebanon became part of many different empires, among them Arab, Persian, Ottoman, Roman, Byzantine, and Crusader.

Spanning over 400 years, the Ottoman Empire controlled Lebanon, followed World War I. This area soon became part of the French Mandate of Syria. In the year 1920, France formed what is known as the State of "Greater Lebanon". At the time, Lebanon was largely occupied by Maronite Christians but also included areas containing many Druzes and Muslims. In the year 1926, Lebanese Republic was formed by France. After this The Republic became a different entity from Syria but still administered under the French Mandate for Syria.

The capital of Lebanon is currently Beirut, the largest city and sometimes referred to by its French name, Beyrouth with a population of around 1.5 million.

Beirut was originally named by the Phoenicians "Bêrūt" which means "The Wells". The first historical reference to Beirut dates from the 15th century BCE, when it is mentioned in a cuneiform tablet called "Amarna letters". These cuneiform

Script tablets are one of the earliest known forms of written expression, mostly diplomatic, between the Egyptian administration and its representatives in Canaan.

Today, Lebanese population speaks primarily Arabic but also French and English. Statistically, most Lebanese Christians speak Arabic and French while the Lebanese Muslim community speaks Arabic and English. A great portion of the Lebanese population also live outside Lebanon, in countries such as South America, Africa, Europe and many Middle Eastern countries.

Lebanon, as a land, has been invaded and occupied by foreign powers for centuries because of it's strategic position in the Middle East. Due to the high number of religions and sects within a very limited geographical location and strong civilization neighborhoods such as Israel and Syria, Lebanon has had many difficulties in unifying it's population and political alliances.

Despite major French and international peace keeping efforts and political restructuring, French style "Republic", Lebanon still suffers from a very unstable environment.

The on-going historical Palestinian and Israeli war, heating up the region has been an additional slow down in the Lebanese political unification and has not been resolved despite all international efforts to this day.

41. ■ Where is the Oldest Arabian City?

Irum is mentioned in ancient scripts, in its Arabic form "Iruma", and is spoken of in folk tales as a trading centre of the Rub' al Khali Desert in the southern part of the Arabian Peninsula. It is the oldest known Arabian city, and it is estimated that it lasted from about 3000 BCE to the first century CE. It became, according to legends, fabulously wealthy from the trade with the coastal regions and central populations of the middle-east and even into Europe. The city became lost to modern history and had been thought by some to be only a mythical tale. The Qur'an says that Irum was a city built by the tribe of Ad, the great-grandchildren of Noah. It was a rich and decadent city.

Irum is mentioned in The Qur'an, chapter 89 (Al-Fajr), verses 6 to 8: "Have you not considered how your Lord dealt with Ad, (The people of) Iruma, possessors of lofty buildings, the like of which were not created in the (other) cities".

The stories tell us that the King of Irum, Shaddad, defied the warnings of the Prophet Hud (in the Bible Eber or Heber), and God destroy the city instantly, driving it into the sands - never to be seen again, becoming a veritable Atlantis of the deserts. The ruins of the city are believed to lie buried somewhere in the sands of Rub' al Khali, an area between Southern Saudi Arabia and Oman. Irum became known to Western literature in "The Book of One Thousand and One Nights", translated originally from Persian language.

The camel trails and old trade routes were already known, rediscovered by an expedition in 1953. The discovery of the ruins of Ubar was made almost by chance in 1992 when a team led by Ranulph Fiennes decided to investigate ruins at the site of Shis'r fort. These remains are believed to be what was left of the 'Atlantis of the Sands' a name given to Irum by T.E. Lawrence (Lawrence of Arabia).

More research and discoveries finally brought Irum out of the realm of myth into history, when tablets were found in the archives of Ebla (an ancient city located in northern Syria, about 55 km southwest of Aleppo) that mentioned Irum by name. In 1993, archaeologists examined photographs taken of the Southern Arabian Peninsula from the space shuttle Challenger, which revealed a buried city along the ancient trade route dating from 2800 BCE TO 100 BCE. Along the eastern edge of Oman and Southern Saudi Arabia in the Dhofar province, these reamins proved to be the city known as The Lost City of Ubar, which is usually identified with Irum.

Additionally, the research program used a remote sensing satellite ground penetrating radar and Landsat program, along with data from NASA and SPOT data to identify old camel trail routes and the points where they converged. Excavations uncovered a fortress which protected the caravan routes and the all-important water source, which was a large limestone cavern underneath the fortress. Evidence of wide-spread trade was found around the site. As the Ubarites (Citizens of Ubar) consumed the water from underground, the water table would fall, leaving the limestone roof and walls of the cavern dry. Without the support of the water, the cavern collapsed between 300-500 AD, destroying the entire city and covering over the water source. After this collapse, the city perished completely and became a legend. Irum is considered to be the oldest city of the Arabian Peninsula and will remain a mystery for many years to come.

42. ■ Where is the Sahara?

Known as the largest hot desert in the world, The Sahara can also be known as the second largest desert after Antarctica. It covers more than 9,000,000 square kilometers, this makes it close to the size of the United States. From north to south the Sahara is between 1,300 and 2,000 km and is at least 4,800 km from east to west. The Sahara is located in North Africa and is estimated to be 2.5 million years old. The word Sahara in English language is from the word as-Sahra, which is the Arabic word that means "desert secret". The first European explorer to travel in the Sahara was Friedrich Horneman in 1805.

The highest part of the desert is at the summit of Mount Koussi in the Tibesti Mountains in Chad, which is 3,415 m high. Some mountain peaks may even have snow in the winter such as Hoggar in Algeria or Aïr Azbine in Nigeria. It has been reported that the tips of these mountains have no more ice for the last few years due to global warming.

Sahara is not a pleasant place to live. Daytime temperature reached 59 Degrees in Azizia, Libya in September 1922. Despite the heat and the tough climatic conditions, there are two permanent rivers running through the Sahara, the Nile River and Niger. Only 200,000 square kilometers of the Sahara desert are fertile oasis, where dates, corn and fruits are grown around the main rivers. This is less than 1% of the overall Sahara !

In spite of it's harsh climates and terrain, there are more than 4 million people living in the Sahara, mostly in Mauritania, Western Sahara, Algeria, Libya and Egypt. The dominant groups of people are Sahrawis, Tuareg and Negroids. The largest Sahara city is Nouakchott, Mauritania's capital. The name Nouakchott is from Berber origin and means "the Shell" or "Place of".

Small animal life of the Sahara includes gerbils, jerboa, cape hare, sand fox, weasel, mongoose and the desert hedgehog. The larger animal population consists of Barbary sheep, Oryx, gazelle, deer, wild ass, baboon, hyena, and the jackal. The bird life counts more than 300 species and are mostly protected by worldwide animal protection agencies.

The most dangerous species of the Sahara are probably scorpions and snakes. The most deadly insect is the mosquito that carries many diseases and blood related infections to humans. Mosquitoes are even more dangerous than wild animals as they operate in the dark and at night and they are lightweight and agile.

I believe the most secret location in the Sahara is located In Northern Chad called Ennedi Massif. In the heart of the Sahara Desert lies a forgotten mountain massif protecting a flora and fauna of breathtaking beauty in its secret canyons. Access to the Ennedi Massif is difficult and only a few rare nomads have been privileged to penetrate the heart of this astounding region, which jealously hides the last evidence that the world is disappearing, the Sahara.

Finally, we should be reminded that the oldest mummy discovered up until modern-day was located in the area of the Ethiopian Sahara. I believe the Sahara has much more to offer and there are possibly many historical treasures hidden and buried in the sand.

43 ■ What is Sahara History?

The Sahara has been inhabited since 6000 BCE. Many civilizations have crossed and lived within it's boundaries. We can divide the Sahara's history into 5 distinctive periods. The Egyptian, The Berber, The Greek, The Urban and the Arab periods.

Egyptian Period: It was during the Egyptian period, approx 6000 BCE that the pre-dynastic Egyptians inhabited the area. While they had chosen the southwest portion of Egypt they maintained their efforts of creating buildings as well as herding animals. During this 6th millennium BCE, there has been documented proof that they have maintained seasonal employment with the Al Fayyum. It was also during this time that they designed their lifestyles focusing on gathering food, by means of hunting animals as well as fishing. Common items that have been found from this time include arrowheads, scrapers, and knives.

Berber Period: During the Berber Period, it was The Phoenicians that began to colonize their kingdoms that span across the Sahara. As they made their settlements, they focused on the area along the coasts, while some chose to remain in the desert. It was around 2500 BCE that the historical version of the Sahara became the dry desert landscape it is today. While some settlements are scattered, usually near an oasis, for the most part it is an uncrossable area. In fact, there is little to no trade or other services available. As mentioned, there are some exceptions in this area, the main one would be the Nile Valley. The Nile remains virtually unpassible at some areas, which has resulted in the difficulties obtaining an established trade, as well as contacting certain areas of inhabitation. In the span of 633 and 530 BCE Hanno the Navigator was the reasons that several Phoenician colonies were started or given strength. However, to this day there are no remains of those ancient colonies to be found.

Greeks Period: Around the time of 500 BCE, the Greeks influences had begun to cross the Sahara, as Greek traders began their treks along the Eastern Coast of the desert. During this time, they began establishing new colonies, while establishing previous trading colonies along the coast of the red sea. While the Carthaginians focused their explorations along the Atlantic coast of the desert. Because of rough waters and a complete lack of other markets, there was never any expanding to the southern portions past Morocco. This meant that only the North and East had areas of civilized inhabitation. For the people who remained on the edge of the centralized states, there was constant fear of attacks from the Berber people.

Urban civilization: Deep in the heart of the Sahara, a new urban civilization began to grow. The Garamantes, began to develop their civilization in the valley known as Wadi al-Ajal around Fazzan, Libya. They were able to build this civilization thanks largely to digging tunnels into the walls of mountains, where they would find ancient waters and use them to water their crops. As their progress continued, they grew more powerful and began to overthrow their neighbors and turned them into slaves, forcing them to maintain their tunnels. While the ancient Romans and Greeks were aware of the Garamantes, they ignored them as nomads. Still, they chose to trade with them, and there are remains of Roman baths located in the Garamantes capital Garama. Once the resources from the mountain became depleted however, they Garamantes Civilization faded and they no longer continued their tunneling efforts.

The Arabs: After the Arab settlement of the Sahara, trade across the desert intensified. The kingdoms of the Sahel, especially the Ghana Empire and the later Mali Empire, grew rich and powerful exporting gold and salt to North Africa. The emirates along the Mediterranean Sea sent south manufactured goods and horses. From the Sahara itself, salt was exported. This process turned the scattered oasis communities into trading centres, and brought them under the control of the empires on the edge of the desert. As Arab civilization was the last to conquer the Sahara, the Arabic language settled across Sahara. This is the main reasons why many African countries speak or understand some dialect of Arabic Language.

This is the final evidence that Arabic Language combined with Islam can unify people of different backgrounds, languages, traditions and cultures even in the harshest place on earth, the Sahara.

References Used in this Book

BOOKS:
The Holy book of Qur'an

The Bible

The Koran: A very short Introduction by Michael Cook

Oxford Dictionary of Islam by john L. Esposito

Jews, Christians, Muslims a Comparative Introduction by John Carrigan

Islam for Dummies by Malcom Clark

The Cambridge Illustrated History of the Islamic World by Ira M. Lapidus

History Of God: The 4000-Year Quest of Judaism, Christianity, and Islam by Karen Armstrong

Understanding Arabs: A Guide for Modern Times by Margaret K. Nydell

History of the Arabs, Revised: 10th Edition by Philip Hitti and Walid Khalidi

CultureShock! United Arab Emirates by Gina Crocetti Benesh

A History of the Arab Peoples by Albert Hourani

WEBSITES:

CIA Fact Book
Google.com
About.com
Americas Global Foundation
Answers.com
Anglik.net
Asinah.net Encyclopedia
BBC and BBC world websites
Britannica.com
FactMonster.com
Ethnologue.com
Infoplease.com
WorldBook.com
TheFreeDictionary.com
Biography.com
Dictionary.com
Omniglot.com
Orbis Latinus on orbilat.com
Reference.com
YourDictionary.com
Economist.com
Wikipedia.com
Wordorigins.org
CNN.com
KhaleejTimes.com

Notes:

Notes: